The Great Western

The Great Western

LEGENDARY LADY OF THE SOUTHWEST

by
BRIAN SANDWICH

The University of Texas at El Paso

Copyright © 1991
Texas Western Press
The University of Texas at El Paso
El Paso, Texas 79968-0633

All rights reserved. No part of this book may be used or reproduced in any manner without written permission of Texas Western Press, except in the case of brief quotations employed in reviews and similar critical works.

First Edition
Library of Congress Catalog Card No. 89-052074
ISBN 0-87404-185-6

 All Texas Western Press books are printed on acid-free paper, meeting the guidelines for permanence and durability of the Committee on Production Guidelines for Book Longevity of the Council on Library Resources.

Sam Chamberlains painting of The Great Western is the only known likeness of her.
Photo by Herb Orth, *Life Magazine*, 1956. Courtesy Time-Life, Inc.

CONTENTS

Acknowledgement
i

CHAPTER 1
"The Great Western"
1

CHAPTER 2
On To Mexico
15

CHAPTER 3
El Paso and the Forty Niners
22

CHAPTER 4
Fort Yuma and the Yuma Crossing
29

CHAPTER 5
Arizona Travels
45

Epilogue
62

Notes
67

Bibliography
74

ACKNOWLEDGEMENTS

I must begin my acknowledgements with a very grateful statement of appreciation to Richard Pearce-Moses of the Arizona Collection at Arizona State University. In spite of what must have seemed an endless barrage of questions, his expertise, professionalism, and kindness were truly reassuring and I am most grateful. Richard Lynch, Susie Sato, Maria Hernandez and all of the wonderful people at the Arizona Historical Foundation, in the library at A.S.U., were equally generous with their time and materials. To Dr. Ben Sacks, I and all students of Arizona history, owe a tremendous debt. The encouragement and help of Aaron and Ruth Cohen, of Guidon Books in Scottsdale, proved to be priceless. Reba Wells of the Arizona Historical Society provided an enthusiasm for the project that was infectious. I wish to thank Jim May, Lynn Roberts and Dave Grale and all at ACES Entertainment in Phoenix for the use of their computer equipment. Al Croke deserves a note of thanks for being my fellow "ghosthunter" and a willing reader and listener throughout this project.

Marshall Trimble, Arizona historian and teacher, first introduced me to Sarah several years ago. His knowledge and willingness to help, patience and friendship mean so much to me, that I, along with the state of Arizona owe him a great deal.

Finally, and most specially, I thank my wonderful wife Jan and my beautiful daughter Jessica. Their love, support, and tolerance throughout this project were the wind beneath my wings and I most gratefully dedicate this book to them.

CHAPTER 1

"The Great Western"

In the sleepy predawn hours of 28 April 1838, crowds began to gather slowly around the waterfront and along the piers of New York City. What had drawn them on that bright spring morning was an announcement that the first steam-driven ships to cross the Atlantic Ocean on a regular schedule were due to arrive. Prior to that day, the only means of ocean travel had been by sailing ship. The schedules and comforts of traveling by ship had been entirely at the whim of the wind and the weather. Steam power promised a new means of providing predictable, speedy comfort on the high seas.

At eleven in the morning, the Staten Island Telegraph announced that the steamship — The Great Western — was soon to enter the harbor. Word spread quickly through the crowd and the number of onlookers approached twenty thousand. The Great Western was the largest ship afloat at the time. Twin, steam-driven paddle wheels churned on each side of her 235-foot-long hull. Two four-hundred-horsepower engines drove her sleek black form through the sea and sent thick black smoke curling from her smoke stack. As she reached the harbor area, small boats swarmed around and the huge crowd sent up cheer after cheer of welcome.[1]

The arrival of regular steamship service from Europe heralded a new age in ocean travel. The sights and sounds of that exciting April morning would remain with everyone who was present that day. The Great Western was unforgettable.

American troops on the beach at Corpus Christi. Photo courtesy Library of Congress.

In 1845 Pres. James K. Polk anticipated trouble with Mexico over the proposed annexation of the Republic of Texas. He ordered Gen. Zachary Taylor to organize an army at Fort Jessup, Louisiana, and then advance into Texas to establish a presence and indicate to Mexico the intention of the United States to hold its new territory.

That fall Taylor mobilized four thousand troops and chose as his destination the white sand beach at Corpus Christi Bay. A trading post known as Kinney's Ranch occupied two dozen buildings at the top of a bluff at the back of the beach.[2] To the front was the cool green water of the bay, whipped into small whitecaps by an almost continuous wind. Beyond the bluff was a vast, mesquite-covered plain. The beach itself curved in a huge crescent shape. To the north was the mouth of the Nueces River, and to the southeast, running for miles along the coast, was Padre Island.

The few occupants of Kinney's Ranch must have gazed in awe as the ships arrived and began to unload wave after wave of armed men. In a matter of days their tiny oceanside outpost was transformed into the largest gathering of army troops since the Revolutionary War. Hundreds of tents in long rows covered the beach for more than a mile, and the peaceful scene that had existed was covered over like a blanket by the gathering warriors.

As winter arrived, their beachfront camp became miserable. The piercing wind drove sleet and rain through the canvas tents. Drinking water turned to ice and unsanitary conditions worsened.[3] Because of the frigid conditions, up to a third of the men became sick, and the staff of medical doctors was kept busy around the clock.[4]

A small town of about two thousand persons had sprung up around Kinney's Ranch. Composed of the camp followers who made a livelihood from the soldiers' paychecks, this hamlet would become the city of Corpus Christi. One soldier noted, "In a short time hundreds of temporary structures were erected on the outskirts of the 'Rancho' and in them, all the cutthroats, thieves, and murderers of the United States and Texas, seem to have congregated."[5] Another soldier present remarked that, in the town of shacks and hastily thrown up framework saloons, "There are no ladies and very few women."[6]

Into this scene of organized chaos rode a woman named Sarah. An article in the Niles National Register of 15 August 1846 decribed this "camp-follower" as belonging "to a class known and recognized in the organization of the army as 'Laundresses,' three of whom are allowed to draw rations in each company, and are required to wash for the soldiers thereof, at a price regulated by a council of officers.... Up to the time the Army marched for the Rio Grande, she performed all her appropriate duties and in addition, kept a 'mess' for the young officers of the regiment."[7] Her duties included, in addition to washing clothes and cooking for the officers, helping to care for the sick and wounded.

Throughout the remainder of her remarkable life she would be referred to in journals and newspapers, and in later reminiscences, as everything from "a ministering angel"[8] to "the greatest whore in the west."[9] Her most striking feature however, was her size:

"An erect and majestic carriage, she glories in a height of six feet ... any soldier might well envy her athletic but graceful form."[10]

"Remarkably large, well proportioned, strong woman of strong nerves and great physical power, capable of enduring great fatigue."[11]

"Tall, large and well made."[12]

"Her masculine arms lifted us one after another off our feet."[13]

And finally, this somewhat unusual way of measuring her height:

"She was an immense woman, would whip most anybody in a rough and tumble fight.... You can imagine how tall she was, she could stand flatfooted and drop these little sugar plums [her nipples] right into my mouth that way."[14]

Imagine the following scene:

A group of half-frozen soldiers huddled around a campfire on the beach one late afternoon, as the ceaseless wind cut through their drizzle-soaked clothes. The rain had let up for a moment, and they were happy just to be outside of the mildewed tents. Despite the cold, the fresh salt air smelled good, and a few errant rays of sunshine streaked through the gray clouds.

As they talked among themselves, one of them mentioned he had heard there was a new laundress over in the officers' area who deserved a second look. Their heads turned to peer toward the wood and earth windbreak that surrounded the officers' tents one hundred yards up the beach from where they sat.

Suddenly, like some vision through the mist, she appeared outside the officers' compound and began to set up her cooking pot for their evening meal. Her long red hair waved in the sea breeze, and she seemed to effortlessly move the heavy iron cooking pot. As they continued to stare in awe-stricken silence, an officer appeared from his tent and engaged her in conversation. The men were further amazed when they realized that, although he was a big man by their standards, she stood nearly a head taller and was certainly as powerful in appearance.

One of the men recovered his speech and said, almost unconsciously: "Lordee! Look at the size of her! Why she's purt' near as big as the Great Western!" The others nodded in mute agreement and a legend was born.

While purely conjecture, the above scenario, or some version of it, no doubt occurred at some point, because in a short time Sarah's past name was forgotten and she was known by all as the "Great Western."[15] Sarah must have not minded the comparison, as several sources state that she called herself "The Western" in later times.

Where she had come from and how she got to that beach is a subject of some conjecture. Lewis Leonidas Allen interviewed Sarah in Matamoros, Mexico, and wrote that "She is of respectable parentage and respectable connection."[16] Her birthplace and date vary with sources. Arthur Woodward, in his dissertation *The Great Western, Amazon of the Army*, states that her burial certificate indicates her birth took place in Clay County, Missouri, in 1813.[17] However, she gave her place of birth as "Tennessee" to the federal census takers in 1850[18] and 1860.[19] Her age also varies on these censuses, listing either 1813 or 1817 as the year of her birth. Finally, there is the curious notation by an unknown hand on her burial plot location card at the the Presidio in San Francisco, which indicates her date of birth as 5 June 1812.[20]

Researching Sarah's past is also complicated by the uncertainty of her maiden name and the identity of her first husband. In an interview with G. N. Allen that occurred two years after Corpus Christi, she refers to Capt. George Lincoln who "enlisted me 6 years ago [1840] at Jefferson Barracks [Missouri] shortly after my first husband joined the regiment."[21] She may have traveled later that year to Florida to fight in the Seminole Indian War. An article written after her death reported that she left "her home in the wilds of Missouri in 1835 or '6 when only twenty years of age [and] accompanied the U. S. troops to Florida, as laundress."[22] Another writer says that she "was always with General Taylors' division; was in Florida, and afterwards there in Mexico."[23] There is no proof of this and unfortunately, no record of anyone mentioning her there.

Who her "first husband" was at the time of her enlistment, is still something of a mystery.[24] Various writers refer to her last name as being: Bourdette, Bouget, Davis, Borginnis, and Bowman.[25] She gave her name as "Sarah Bourjette" on the 1850 census. Returning to Lewis Allen's interview, he refers to her as:

> The wife of an orderly sergeant.... In early life she married a soldier, as young ladies will do when they take it into their heads. Her husband being necessarily called away from home, and deprived of the society of his family for a long period, and often upon the frontiers in imminent peril, exposed to dangers, and doomed to undergo hardships, true to a woman's nature, she determined to accompany him to camp; hence, she emphatically chose the profession of arms for her future calling.[26]

Whatever her true name at Corpus Christi, she and her husband were apparently separated on 8 March 1846 when the order finally came to move south into Mexico. The army marched overland to a new camp near Matamoros, twenty-seven miles up the Rio Grande. The women and sick were to be transported by ship and along the coast Point Isabel, where Taylor would gather supplies.

The *Spirit of the Times* newspaper of 25 July 1846 reports in an earlier copy of the same article that appeared in the *Niles National Register*:

> A very few [women] procured ponies and followed their husbands on their tedious and arduous march. Not so with "THE GREAT WESTERN". Her husband was sent by water, whether on duty or for disability, I am unable to learn; but she, true to her character, declaring that the "boys" (young officers of her mess) must have somebody to take care of them, purchased a mule and cart, packed her luggage, cooking utensils, and supplies mounted behind her donkey, with whip in hand, and displayed upon the whole route qualities and attainments which the best teamster in the train might have envied. During the whole journey she kept up the "mess" a relief from the burdens of which, is the greatest boon to an officer on the march.[27]

As the move toward the Rio Grande began, three thousand soldiers trudged through a carpet of yellow and blue wildflowers that covered the Texas prairie. A soldier recalled that "A delicious fragrance filled the air, and the whole surface of the earth as far as the eye could reach, seemed covered with a beautiful carpet."[28] The bluebonnets also hid Texas rattlesnakes, and soldiers had to be careful where they placed their feet. After three days the column encountered an enormous herd of wild horses. The herd extended from horizon to horizon, running at full speed with thick manes and tails flying in the wind. U. S. Grant, who was at the time a captain, reported, "There is no estimating the number of animals in it. I have no idea that all could have been coralled in the state of Rhode Island or Delaware at one time. If they had been, the pasturage would have given out the first day."[29]

Next came a parched desert where the men were smothered by the hot dry climate. Dust rose in clouds and lips and skin were burned by the unrelenting sun. The sand was soft and warm, and the men sank to their ankles in it. The Mexicans had burned what little grass grew in this place, and as the men marched the ashes were churned up, making the men "resemble Africans."[30]

Finally, the thirsty column approached a stream called the Arroyo Colorado. The banks were thirty feet high, so engineers were brought forward to hack an access down to the water. As the troops struggled forward and came to a halt among the thickets, a group of Mexicans appeared on the opposite shore and began to make threatening noises, rustle the bushes, blow bugles, and stir up dust clouds. Mexican officers appeared and warned Taylor not to cross or he would be fired upon. Undaunted, Taylor continued to have his roadway constructed to the water's edge and prepared to cross.

Tensions rose as the men realized that this could be the moment of truth. Throughout that day preparations continued for what seemed certain to be the opening volley of war.[31]

The Great Western was about to perform her first legendary act. Sarah idolized Zachary Taylor. She was absolutely confident in his ability as a leader and in the soldiers ability to win the impending war. Throughout the conflict she would time and again express her patriotism and faith in the outcome. Like Taylor, she was apparently unimpressed by the Mexicans' little show across the river and, rushing up to the general, announced coolly that "If the general would give her a strong pair of tongs [pants] she would wade that river and whip every scoundrel that dared show himself."[32] This display of bravery must have had quite an effect on the men and, led by Gen. William Jenkins Worth, they charged through the shallow water toward the

General Zachary Taylor whom Sarah followed throughout the Mexican-American war. Photo from Library of Congress.

thickets on the opposite shore. The Mexican "hordes" however, had already vanished and their bluff had been called. Sarah's little speech had won the admiration of the men and their respect would remain and grow. The press reported the incident, and she quickly became a symbol of patriotic womanhood.

Lewis Allen reports that, during the crossing of the stream, Sarah "rendered great assistance; and in one instance saved the lives of a number of soldiers who were crossing in a flatboat — which sank while she and her children were on it"[33] Sarah, as far is known, never gave birth to a child. She is however, documented on several instances as having taken in orphaned children. It would be highly unlikely that she had intentionally brought along children during the march, so if Allen is correct about children being present, they must have been someone else's.

After crossing the Arroyo Colorado, the column continued on the last thirty miles toward the destination of Matamoros on the Rio Grande. At a point about ten miles from Matamoros and ten miles from Point Isabel on the coast, Taylor split the command.[34] The men's spirits had been buoyed by their "victory" back at the river, and they marched four abreast, feeling invincible as the countryside became beautiful again with flowers and grass reappearing.[35] Before the final push to the river, however, Taylor needed to protect his lifeline to the outside at Point Isabel. He did not want to risk having his supply line cut and, after his long march, he needed to restock and make sure all was well there. The column resumed its march after his return. On 28 March 1846 at 10:30 A.M., they arrived across the river from Matamoros, Mexico.

Located on the south side of the Rio Grande, the town looked to the poetic Captain W. S. Henry "like a fairy vision before our enraptured eyes."[36] Lush gardens surrounded the neat white stucco houses, and at sundown the women of the town would come out to the river and bathe along the water's edge. The military bands of each side sent up nightly serenades. Mexican peddlers moved freely among the Americans selling their wares, and all seemed deceivingly calm.

Wise old Taylor was not fooled by the apparent friendliness of the Mexicans and immediately began to throw up a six-sided fort. While the two sides postured and coyly pretended all was well, tensions steadily rose within the walls of "Fort Texas." Diplomatic relations were limited at best, and several minor incidents culminated with Captain Thornton and sixty three of his men being attacked on 25 April 1846. Sixteen men were killed and the rest were captured. Zachary Taylor sent a terse message to Pres. James Polk stating that "Hostilities may now be considered as commenced." The United States and Mexico were at war.[37]

Finishing touches were added, and the fort was hastily completed. With nine-foot-high walls and fifteen-foot parapets, its six sides presented a stout resistance to the Mexicans. Gun emplacements were constructed around the edges, and cannon were aimed across the river at the Mexican batteries. Bomb-proof shelters were constructed for the ammunition, as well as for the sick and wounded.[38]

Taylor however, had more troubles. Mexican troops were reported to be moving toward his supply base at Point Isabel, which would threaten his lifeline should a long siege set in. He would have to move back and protect his base, or risk being cut off without supplies. On 1 May he decided to move most of the men to Point Isabel to secure it; then they would return to Fort Texas. He chose Maj. Jacob Brown to stay at the fort with five hundred men, the women, and the sick, with orders to hold the position at all costs. Brown was not to attempt any offensive action, or to leave the fort for any reason and was to conserve his ammunition as much as possible. If it appeared that his men were in danger of losing the fort, they were to fire the eighteen pound guns at regular intervals as a signal to the troops at Point Isabel. Brown had a moat dug around the perimeter of the fort, and preparations continued throughout the next day.[39] The Americans noted much activity that morning across the river in Matamoros. Bells rang and priests could be seen going about the city blessing the soldiers at each battery. This was taken as a certain omen of an impending attack. At five o'clock, on the morning of 3 May 1846, the bombardment began.[40]

The Great Western was among the ten or twelve women left behind in the bastion. When the bombardment commenced, the women were moved into the "bomb-proofs" with the ammunition and the sick. The women were put to work sewing sandbags to shore up the walls of the fort and protect the artillery men. Sarah's indomitable spirit shone as she set up her cook fires and kettle near the center of the fort and began to prepare breakfast as usual. The *Spirit of the Times* reported:

> When the hour arrived for breakfast, but few expected the luxury which awaited them. The mess was well attended to, as if nothing but a morning drill with blank cartridges had come off, and in addition, a large supply of hot coffee was awaiting the thirsty, who had but to call and partake without distinction of rank. To some of the artillerymen who were unable to leave their guns, the beverage was carried by this "ministering angel" and, as may be believed, no belle of Orleans, as much as she might be admired and beloved, ever met a more gracious reception.[41]

According to Lewis Allen, Sarah may have been a "ministering angel," but she was not without some limitations. Allen states that when the bombardment became exceptionally heavy, and the men began to ask her to bring the food to them along the walls:

> She became very much offended and indignant at their conduct in making such a demand. After she had run such great risks and periled her life, to demand her to expose her life still more, in carrying food from her tent to them, was asking a little too much, and she begged to be excused, and upbraided them in very severe terms for their want of courage.[42]

During the first day alone, more than fifteen hundred shells exploded. Miraculously, a sergeant named Wiegart was the only man killed.[43] The Mexicans were using badly outdated guns and ammunition. The shells shot at the Americans were balls made of bronze or iron with lit fuses on them. This type of bomb would explode and send its force upward instead of outward, causing little real damage unless it scored a direct hit. At night the lighted bombs looked like "firey comets," and the men would be able to simply sidestep the incoming balls.[44]

The Great Western • 11

Drawing of Major Jacob Brown being mortally wounded during the bombardment. Copied from Frost, John. *Pictorial History of Mexico and the Mexican War*. Richmond, Va., Harrold & Murray, 1848. p.219. Courtesy of the Institute of Texan Cultures at San Antonio.

The fire of the artillery was kept up almost incessantly until dinner hour — a soldier's dinner hour is 1 o'clock — then the good and generous woman again provided for those who were almost utterly exhausted and worn out, a delicious dish of bean soup. This bean soup is declared by the Mexicans to be the foundation of that invincible spirit which they have seen so strikingly displayed by the Yankee soldiers. This she distributed again, without money and without price.[45]

The bombardment continued to rain shells on the fort for the next seven days and nights, a total of 160 hours of nearly continuous assault. On 6 May, the third day of the bombardment, Major Brown was hit. A falling shell struck his right leg and nearly tore it off. He was carried to one of the bomb-proofs, but gallantly told those who escorted him, "Men, go to your duties, stand by your posts; I am but one among you."[46] He clung to life for three days in the stifling air of the bomb proof and finally succumbed on 9 May.

After Major Brown was killed, Capt. E. S. Hawkins assumed command. General Arista of the Mexican army sent a request for surrender to Hawkins and received the terse reply, "I must respectfully decline to surrender my forces to you."[47]

This response apparently renewed the Mexicans' vigor, as they redoubled their bombardment and began surrounding and enclosing the besieged fort with more than five thousand men. The Americans, though low on ammunition, managed to do enough damage by firing accurately that they intimidated the enemy into keeping a respectful distance. Sarah asked for and received a musket, "expressing her determination to have full satisfaction whenever the enemy should dare approach within range of her piece."[48]

The Western continued to serve her meals and carry coffee by the bucketful to the men along the walls. Lewis Allen wrote that "the cannonballs, bullets and shot… were falling thick and fast around her. She continued to administer to the wants of the wounded and dying; at last the siege became so hot that a bullet passed through her bonnet and another through her bread tray." He added that her meals were always on time and "always of the best the market afforded."[49]

General Taylor, twenty-seven miles away at Point Isabel, had heard the distant thunder of the thousands of exploding shells at Fort Texas on 6 May. The previous several days he had been fighting his way through the Mexican armies at Palo Alto and at Resaca De La Palma on the road back to Matamoros, bringing needed supplies. Finally, on the morning of 9 May, the garrison was ecstatic to see General Arista's troops fleeing before the charging army of General Taylor. That evening, as the band played "Yankee Doodle" and the occupants cheered, the fort was relieved.

Some 2,700 shells had been fired at Fort Texas over seven days with the loss of Major Brown and Sergeant Wiegart and the wounding of thirteen privates as the only casualties.[50] Against almost unbelievable odds estimated at ten to one, the small group of men and women had held their first foothold in the war with Mexico. The fort was renamed Fort Brown to honor the fallen leader, and the town which was to grow around it, Brownsville, also honors him.

The story of Sarah's coolness and courage under fire quickly spread and began to appear in newspapers throughout the country. Besides being The Great Western, she was now the Heroine of Fort Brown. Her fame was sealed when Lt. Braxton Bragg of the artillery rose to offer a toast at a party that was being given a delegation from Louisiana in Matamoros shortly after the battle. He toasted the Heroine of Fort Brown and said that

> During the whole of the bombardment, the wife of one of the soldiers, whose husband was ordered with the army to Point Isabel, remained in the fort, and though the shot and shells were constantly flying on every side, she disdained to seek shelter in the bomb-proofs, but labored the whole time cooking and taking care of the soldiers without the least regard to her own safety. Her bravery was the admiration of all who were in the Fort, and she has thus acquired the name of "The Great Western".[51]

The room erupted in cheers and wild applause as glasses were smashed against the walls. Reporters present hastily recorded the events, and Sarah was now a national heroine.

Cover of a booklet published during the Mexican-American war that shows a stylized drawing of Sarah at Fort Brown. Photo from Library of Congress

CHAPTER 2

On To Mexico

On 18 May, after burying the dead and moving the wounded to Point Isabel, Taylor crossed into Matamoros. Other than the toast by Bragg at the Louisiana delegation party, there is no specific mention of The Great Western in Matamoros. Based on her later pattern, it is assumed that she set up a restaurant or hotel there to supplement her income as a laundress. She remained through the summer of 1846.

On 6 July Taylor began to move up the Rio Grande about one hundred miles toward the town of Camargo. By mid-September, the army had turned south and was twenty miles outside of Monterrey near the town of Marin. The Great Western had apparently left Matamoros sometime in late August in pursuit of the column, and Samuel C. Reid reported her on 16 September 1846 in his journal.

> The Heroine of Fort Brown or "The Great Western" is in the crowd. She drives two Mexican Ponies in a light wagon and carries the apparatus and necessaries for her mess which now numbers about a dozen young officers.[1]

Taylor's army moved on toward Monterrey and on 24 September, after a four-day battle in which more than five hundred Americans were killed, they occupied the town. Sarah opened a place called The American House that supplied food, drink, lodging, and women to the soldiers.[2] She must not have had a very permanent setup, however, as when Taylor moved sixty miles southwest toward the town of Saltillo in November, Sarah prepared to move, too. She left some-

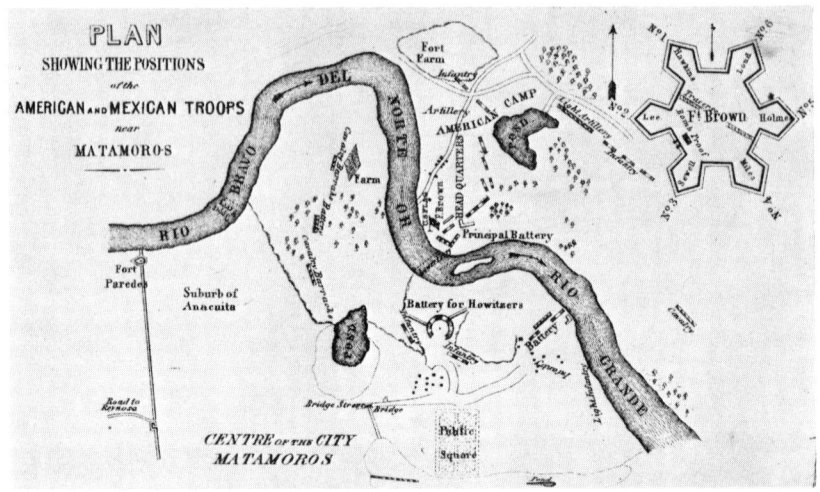

The battle of Fort Brown where Sarah first achieved national attention.
Photo courtesy Library of Congress.

time in late December and was noticed by Benjamin Franklin Scribner as he traveled with his regiment at a point halfway to Saltillo on 30 December 1846. He noted the excitement that her arrival caused and described her as having "the appearance of an Amazon, being tall, muscular, and majestic in her expression." Scribner also noted her heroics at Fort Brown and added that "She issued out coffee to the men while the bombs were falling all around her."[3]

Saltillo was taken without a fight and Sarah quickly established another American House. The city was nearly twice as large as Monterrey and business was good for her in January 1847.

Soon reports began to filter in that Gen. Santa Anna had decided to crush Taylor's army and was massing troops for a push toward Buena Vista about seven miles south of Saltillo. Taylor's spies confirmed that twenty thousand Mexican soldiers were marching feverishly to rout the army of occupation of the United States. Taylor had only 4,759 men, most of whom had never been in battle, and he prepared to make his stand.[4]

On 22 February Santa Anna sent a message to Taylor informing him that he was surrounded and outnumbered: "I wish to save you from a catastrophe, and for that purpose give you this notice, in order that you may surrender at discretion."[5]

Taylor had no intention of surrendering and sent Santa Anna the message: "Sir- in reply to your note of this date, summoning me to surrender my force at discretion, I beg leave to say that I decline acceding to your request. With high respect, I am sir, your Obedient Servant, Z. Taylor."[6]

The battle of the next two days was a back-and-forth clash of power. Taylor's troops, though overwhelmed by the far superior numbers of Santa Anna, held on with luck and desperation and succeeded in holding their ground. Through the confusion and smoke Sarah once again made herself useful. She was at her restaurant in Saltillo at one point during the long battle when some of Taylor's troops panicked and ran. George Washington Trahern, a Texan who was in the battle, recalled the scene:

> There was a big woman they called the Great Western. She was a great nurse and always went with Taylor's Army. She stood six feet two; she was a great nurse and would always get up at any time of night to get one something to eat- kept a sort of restaurant; they all knew her, and the boys tell about one of the Indianans,...[running from the field of battle so fast that]...a jack rabbit broke up, and he passed the jack like he was standing, went into Saltillo and rushed right down to sort of headquarters for everybody, the Great Westerns', and he came running in breathless and told the Great Western that Gen. Taylor was whipped and the army was all cut to pieces, and the Mexicans under full headway for Saltillo. She just drew off and hit him between the eyes and knocked him sprawling; says "You damned son of a bitch, there ain't Mexicans enough in Mexico to whip old Taylor." She says, "You just spread that report and I'll beat you to death."[7]

The remainder of the deserters had second thoughts and, preferring the Mexicans to Sarah, quickly returned to battle. Sarah also appeared at the battlefield and made herself useful as a nurse for Dr. Charles M. Hitchcock. She carried coffee out to the troops and helped in caring for the wounded, actually carrying some men from the field.[8] Capt. George Lincoln of the Eighth Regiment was killed in this battle. G. N. Allen noted Sarah's reaction:

> It is said that when the news arrived of the death of Capt. Lincoln, the "Heroine of Fort Brown" was much affected, and fell upon a chair and wept like a child. "You knew the Captain well, did you not Mrs. Bourdette?" said a person present. "Know him!" said she, wiping the big tears from her browned face with her greasy apron. "Know him! — I didn't know any one else. It was he enlisted me six years ago, in Jefferson Barracks, shortly after my first husband joined the regiment — and we have lived together, that is he has eat at my table all the time since. But, poor dear man, I must go and see to him this very night, lest them rascally greasers should strip him, and not knowing him, I could not give him a decent burial."
>
> Off she went to the blood-stained battlefield, and sought among the dead and dying till she found out the corpse of the brave Captain, which she brought to Saltillo and had decently interred.[9]

Sarah obviously had a deep devotion to Captain Lincoln, and she continued to display her affection several days later when his horse was offered for sale at auction.

> When the first bid was announced, the canteen woman, honored with the soubriquet of "The Heroine of Fort Brown" with whom Lincoln was a especial favorite, stepped forward and said that a man who offered seventy five dollars for a horse like that could not want it — that she would give two hundred and fifty dollars for the animal, and at that price it was knocked off to her. When asked what occasion she had for the horse, she declared her intention to keep it till an opportunity offered of forwarding it to Lincoln's mother, for whom she designed it as a present. She afterwards relinquished the horse to the Kentucky Regiment by whom he was presented to the family of the deceased and forwarded to Boston.[10]

Sarah returned to Saltillo and continued to run her American House. It seems to have been, as Trahern described, "a sort of headquarters for everybody." The soldiers would meet there and could find entertainment, food, girls, and rooms for rent. Fortunately, several of those who visited her place kept journals which mention her.

Col. Sam Curtis of the Third regiment of Ohio Volunteers wrote on 6 April 1847:

> Moved into the city and got a room at the American kept by a woman who seems to be a part of the army. ["Mrs. Bourjette" is written between the lines]. She is commonly called "The Great Western" for her size. She is nearly 6 feet high and well proportioned. She distinguished herself at Fort Brown during the Bombardment in attending the sick and wounded and is said to be a useful soldier. She has several servants, Negroes and Mexicans, and she knocks them about like children. While I am writing, she is watering her horse, a fine white horse that Lincoln was killed on.[11]

On 29 April Curtis makes reference to the Western's provision of female companionship. He "remained in town during the night and paid $2.50 for my entertainment at the boarding house of the Great Western."[12]

On 23 April Lt. Herman Humphrey of the Third Indiana Volunteers arrived at Saltillo and checked into the American House. His journal notes that Sarah had been with General Taylor and "rendered great service in the battles of the Rio Grande and Monterrey in taking care of the wounded soldiers." He described her as being "masculine in appearance and manners, though possessing feminine sympathies and kindness of heart."[13]

Dr. Frederick A. Wislizenus was in Saltillo on 23 May 1847 and noted in his journal that he stayed at Sarah's hotel and added that her "fearless behaviour during the Battle of Buena Vista was highly praised; she dressed many wounded soldiers on that day, and even carried them out of the thickest fight.[14]

Business apparently was good at Sarah's place and she did well. Things must have gotten out of hand occasionally, as an order regarding her establishment was issued as Special Order No.517 from Headquarters, Buena Vista on 17 June 1847 and signed by Irwin McDowell, "By command of Brigr. Genl. Wool." The order read:

> Mrs. Bouget, having by permission of the General established a Boarding House in the vicinity of Camp for the accommodation of the officers — it is to be well understood

that this permission is to be continued on condition that there shall not be a drop of liquor of any kind sold or kept at the establishment. A sentinel will be posted at the Rancho occupied as above, and will be instructed not to permit, under any pretense whatever, soldiers, Teamsters, citizens or women (other than the servants of Mrs. Bouget) to come near the buildings. After sundown the Building will be closed to all whatever. [15]

On 18 July 1848, five months after the signing of the Treaty of Guadalupe Hidalgo ending the war, the command of Maj. Laurence P. Graham, with Bvt. Lt. Col. John Washington commanding the detachment, moved out of Walnut Springs bound for California. They went into camp near Arista Mills and the following morning were preparing to leave when Sarah arrived, riding a horse and leading three wagons. She approached Colonel Washington to ask if she could join the column.[16]

In July of 1848 Colonel Washington had issued an order from his Monterrey headquarters that forbade anyone who was not either employed by the army, or directly connected with it, to travel with the soldiers. Thus, the only way Sarah could accompany the group was to

> marry one of the Dragoons, and be mustered in as a laundress.... Her ladyship gave the military salute and replied, "All right Major, I'll marry the whole Squadron and you thrown in but what I go along." Riding along the front of the line she cried out, "Who wants a wife with fifteen thousand dollars, and the biggest leg in Mexico! Come my beauties, don't all speak at once — who is the lucky man?"[17]

Fifteen thousand dollars must have seemed like a fortune to men who were paid seven dollars a month. Nevertheless, they hesitated and

> At first, no one seemed disposed to accept the offer. Finally Davis of Company E said, "I have no objections to making you my wife, if there is a clergyman here to tie the knot." With a laugh the heroine replied, "Bring your blanket to my tent tonight and I will learn you to tie a knot that will satisfy you I reckon!' Such was the morals of the army in Mexico.

Mrs. Davis, nee Borginnis went down on E Company books as "Laundress" and drew rations as such.[18]

Sarah "Davis" traveled northwest with her group over the next two months to the town of Chihuahua. Sixteen miles outside Chihuahua they reached the town of Sacramento. There, Lieutenant Colonel Washington's command split off and headed north toward Santa Fe, while Major Graham headed off toward California with the remainder.
In mid-September

> After several days' march from Sacramento we reached a branch of the Rio Yaqui, the banks of which for miles were covered with peach trees, full of ripe delicious fruit. A large well armed party from New Mexico was encamped here engaged in collecting and drying the fruit for the Santa Fe market.[19]

Sarah's attention wandered:

> With the party from New Mexico was a man of remarkable size and strength. Madame Sarah Borginnis Davis, the "Great Western," saw this Hercules while he was bathing and conceived a violent passion for his gigantic proportions. She sought an interview and with blushes "told her love." The Samson, nothing loth, became the willing captive to this modern Delilah, who straightaway kicked Davis out of her affections and tent, and established her elephantine lover in full possession without further ceremony.[20]

Sam Chamberlain painted the only known likeness of Sarah in existence. It shows her in front of a bar, wearing a red silk dress. She is drawing a pistol from her belt and is preparing to throw a Mexican soldier out of her establishment. Chamberlain recognized her immediately when she rode up to ask permission to join the troop, so he must have met her before, possibly in Saltillo. It is likely that this is a scene of the interior of her American House in Saltillo.[21]

CHAPTER 3

El Paso and the Forty Niners

Over the next eight months nothing is heard from Sarah. How long she stayed with her "elephantine lover" is unknown. The only clue as to what she had been doing comes from the journal of Lt. Henry Chase Whiting, who was with the U. S. Corps of Topographical Engineers. His group had left San Antonio, Texas, in February 1849 to locate a lower road to El Paso along the Rio Grande. They arrived in the small settlement that would become El Paso, Texas, in April of 1849. On 12 April they crossed over the Rio Grande to El Paso Del Norte (now Cuidad Juarez) on the Mexican side. As they arrived in Mexico, they encountered the Great Western as she headed the opposite direction toward the United States in a canoe. She was so elated at meeting American officers that she embraced them and "Her masculine arms lifted us one after another off our feet." She told Whiting that she had been "left sick in Chihuahua by Major Graham's command" and had experienced much "suffering and hardship." She intended to cross into Texas and "await the arrival of the army."[1]

Paso Del Norte was a town whose population lived mostly on the southern or Mexican side of the river where it cuts a fertile, green swath through the barren desert and mountains. A Mexican, Juan Maria Ponce de Leon, had received a grant to land on both sides of the river in 1827; with the exception of a few of his hired hands' pitching a hut on the northern side for occasional use, there was little activity on that side.[2] A town had existed on the southern side since the late 1600s. It had enjoyed steady growth and yet remained a basically quiet town in northern Mexico. Three things happened in 1848 that changed the town forever.

On 24 January 1848 gold was discovered in California, on the American River at a place called Sutter's Mill. A river of humanity responded to the discovery, and the "Golden Gate" was blown open by a tidal wave of forty-niners. People sold everything they had and charged off into the great plains in a wild rush toward the riches they knew were waiting for them in the west. Ill-prepared for burning deserts, vast treeless plains, and incredibly high mountains blocked by raging blizzards, thousands suffered incredible hardships and died in the quest for gold. The southern route offered an all-weather course and quickly became one of the main arteries to California. From El Paso, travelers followed the Gila River on west.

One week after the discovery of gold in California, on 2 February 1848, the Treaty of Guadelupe Hidalgo was signed ending the Mexican War. With those signatures the Rio Grande became, in addition to a mighty river, an international boundary line. The Pass of the North now led into another country and the town was divided.

The third event that changed El Paso forever was General Orders 58, issued in Washington, which ordered federal troops to El Paso.[3] Various reconnaissance parties were sent out to locate the best routes into El Paso and mobilize troops. Washington felt that, because of the proximity of the Pass to Mexico, troops were needed to protect the westward migrating Americans who were descending on the place. Lieutenant Whiting was on one of those reconnaissance parties when he spotted Sarah on her way to El Paso.

As the hordes descended on the pass, they brought hard times with them. As many as four thousand immigrants were in the pass in August of 1848. The demands for food, shelter, and necessities pressed the limits of the meager village.[4]

Added to the troubles of the people were the Indians who raided the unprotected travelers with regularity. The townspeople on the Mexican side were held virtual captives by the warriors, unable to tend their crops or supply any needs to the growing settlement on the American side. With the eye of a good business woman, Sarah moved to the fertile north side and began to ply her established trade of "hotel keeper." Whiting had noted her crossing over on 12 April "to await the arrival of the army." She probably expected, due to her past record, to find some friends among the men, and she planned to simply get herself established and wait for "her boys" to arrive. By the time they did, she would have a hotel set up to meet all of "their needs."

In late April the first mention of her enterprise came from John S. "Rip" Ford. He and Robert S. Neighbors, two Texas Rangers, were commissioned by the merchants of Austin to locate a route for their trade with the newest American town at the pass. They took two months to make the journey along what became known as the upper road. They arrived in a near-starved condition, but soon recovered and decided to have a look around. Ford reported in his memoirs:

> On our side, an American woman, known as the Great Western, kept a hotel. She was very tall, large and well made. She had the reputation of being something of the roughest fighter on the Rio Grande; and was approached in a polite, if not humble manner by all of us — the writer in particular.[5]

The growing village on the American side of the river was known at this time as Ponce's Ranch. A trader named Benjamin Franklin Coons saw opportunity and bought the ranch from Ponce de Leon in June of 1849. Because of continuing Indian trouble and the crush of the incoming forty-niners, Ponce de Leon was probably happy to part with it. The place became known as Coons Ranch or Franklin, and Coons added a tavern and blacksmith shop and ran advertisements in New Mexican and Texas newspapers promoting his ability to meet all of the traveler's needs. Sarah joined in partnership with Coons and became part-owner of a hotel-restaurant-store that was located along the plaza.[6] Eventually the building would become the Central Hotel.[7] This business qualifies Sarah in several accounts as the first Anglo female resident of what would become El Paso, Texas.[8]

At some point late that spring, Col. Sam Whiting led an expedition along the Lower Road. It was a disastrous experience for all who participated. Whiting was totally inexperienced, yet managed to convince a hundred men to follow him across some of the most barren land in Texas. With inadequate supplies and little or no idea of how to follow a trail, they marched off into what seemed an endless expanse of desert.[9] It is a miracle that any of them survived what became a six-month journey, yet most did, including Augustus W. Knapp, who later would write about his experience. As the near-dead members of the party staggered into Franklin, the tiny burg looked to Knapp to be "paradise itself, so beautiful did it seem after our long, desolate tramp."[10] After recovering for several days, his companions elected to cross over to Paso Del Norte on the Mexican side. Knapp however, was stricken ill and in a few days "was totally unable to help myself." He said farewell to his companions and lay down in a little hut by the river, unsure how he would survive.

As he lay contemplating death, he gazed out to see coming toward him what must have seemed an incredible vision. It was a vision he recognized — "The Great Western." He described Sarah as "being of remarkable stature (over six feet) and strength in proportion," adding that she "took it upon herself to carry in wounded soldiers during and after the battles, and thus became known far and wide." She discovered him in his hut by the river, "and upon learning that I was an American took me in charge, brought me all the necessary remedies at hand, and prepared food that I could eat when able. Thus I had every care and attention that it was possible to obtain under the circumstances."[11]

Life in Franklin must have been a very hard existence. Low supplies, the constant raiding of Indians, and the influx of people meant that only the hardy would survive. Knapp was certainly impressed with Sarah's ability to flourish and prosper under such circumstances. She "kept a kind of inn, being able to hold her own under all circumstances. She was held in dread by the Mexicans who lived about there; and as she was usually armed whenever she went across the Rio Grande to El Paso, no one ever thought of troubling her." Even the Indians "seemed to hold her in perfect awe, and had a superstition that she was a supernatural being."[12]

The raids continued on the Mexican side and, at one point, a few Indians crossed over and came up to Knapp as he lay in his hut. On finding he was an American, they spared his life, but noted that, had Knapp been a Mexican, he would have been killed.[13] Realizing he was not safe, Sarah moved her patient to her hotel where he was able to watch a parade of unusual characters pass daily through her door.

Knapp recovered and moved on, but Sarah stayed at Franklin. Thousands of travelers must have seen and met her or visited her hotel in the tiny town over the next six months. Certainly, in addition to supplying food and board to the travelers, it is probable that she also held the post of madam.

H. Gordon Frost, in his history of prostitution in El Paso, *The Gentleman's Club*, refers to Sarah as "the first madam/prostitute of record to appear on the El Paso scene."[14] The harsh realities of the frontier dictated a different set of morals and occasionally produced a type of character known as "the prostitute with a heart of gold." Sarah proved over and over to be a very good businesswoman and would certainly not turn down any opportunity to profit, but she also repeatedly showed a true compassion for the less fortunate around her. Considering her past displays of character and the later documentation of her activities, likely prostitution was a sideline in El Paso.

Several travelers mention staying at her hotel. In July of 1849, Lewis B. Harris wrote a letter to his brother in which he mentioned her. "We found the far-famed Great Western at this place on our side of the river. She was celebrated in the Mexican War and did good service in a number of battles. She is six feet one inch in height, and well proportioned. She treated us with much kindness."[15]

C. C. Cox, in his diary of 10 July 1849, wrote that "property on this side of the River was recently purchased by Mr. Coon, a trader from Missouri. He also has a large store. Among the residents of the place is numbered 'The Great Western', a female notorious in the late war."[16]

In June of 1849 Maj. Jefferson Van Horne began to march with six companies of soldiers and 275 wagons loaded with supplies to establish a military presence at the pass. After a three month trip from San Antonio covering 673 miles, they arrived in El Paso. Coons had anticipated this opportunity and leased his buildings to the Army. Sarah stayed a while and profited from the presence of the growing population, but things had changed at the pass. Civilization began to arrive with the army and supplies became easier to procure, although there were never enough to accommodate the incredible influx of people. Perhaps the continuing stress of getting enough goods to stay in business was too much, or maybe the new army regulations put too many restrictions on her. Sarah was used to being at the front edge of civilization, and it seemed that the mass of transients passing through were leaving her behind. Their tales of gold-filled streets in California may have tempted her.

For whatever reason, she left El Paso, probably around the beginning of 1850. By December of 1850 she was in Socorro, New Mexico. Her name, "Sarah Bourjette," appears on the United States census taken there.[17] She gave her age as thirty-three, her birthplace as Tennessee and, in the column "persons over 21 years of age who cannot read or write," there is a check by her name. She was living with Juan Duran, who is shown incorrectly as a thirty-eight-year-old *female*. Five Skinner children, Margaret, Diana, Fanny, Caroline and Nancy, also shared the household. Their ages ranged from two to sixteen. The four youngest were born in Illinois and the oldest in Texas. Two servants were also listed, as well as a boy who probably belonged to them. The Skinner children may have been orphaned during the trip to El Paso and good-hearted Sarah took them in, or possibly she simply met them in Socorro and struck up a friendship that lasted. At any rate, Nancy would continue to be a part of Sarah's life, and later would refer to her as "mother."

On another page of the same census are listed the soldiers who were stationed at Socorro. One is listed as a soldier born in Denmark, whose occupation was "Sergeant U.S.A." He was twenty-four years old and, though no record of an "official" marriage can be found, Sarah took his last name and was known as his wife. For the next sixteen years they shared the hardships of the southwestern frontier. The sergeant's name was Albert Bowman.

Maj. Samuel Heintzelman who commanded Fort Yuma and knew Sarah well.
Photo courtesy Arizona Historical Foundation, Tempe.

CHAPTER 4

Fort Yuma and the Yuma Crossing

What little is known of Albert Bowman is pieced together from his pension records and the regimental returns of Company E, Second Dragoons.[1] Though the census of 1850 indicated his place of birth as Denmark, he would give Brunswick, Germany, as his birthplace on all subsequent documentation. He enlisted in the army on 4 December 1847 in New York City and served with the Second Dragoons in the Mexican War under Col. W. S. Harney. He joined Company "E" in June of 1849, traveled to Santa Fe in October, and arrived in Socorro in November. The company stayed at Socorro until September of 1851, when it went on to Fort Conrad. In February of 1852 he was transferred to Fort Fillmore and, in March, went on to Fort Webster. Sarah may have stayed behind to work in the hospital at Fillmore.

Sylvester W. Matson was a soldier at Fort Webster when Sarah arrived on 9 May. He was quite impressed by her and made the following notation in his diary:

> Today we are reinforced by a renowned female character. They call her "Doctor Mary." Her other name is the "Great Western." She is accompanied by Major Morris and Lieutenant O'Bannion. This woman is a giantess. She is over seven feet tall. She gets a pension for life from the United States for bravery in action during the recent war between the United States and Mexico. At the siege of Matamoros, where a piece of artillery had been silenced by loss of the men she took the place of one of them at the gun and kept it firing

The Yuma crossing as it appeared when Sarah arrived. Photo courtesy of Special Collections, University of Arizona Library.

during the balance of the battle, doing considerable execution with this cannon. She also successfully defended herself with a saber when attacked while serving the gun. She slew a Mexican who cut her across the cheek with his saber. She boasts a large scar on her cheek from this wound. She appears here modest and womanly not withstanding her great size and attire. She has on a crimson velvet waist, a pretty riding skirt and her head is surmounted by a gold laced cap of the Second Artillery. She is carrying pistols and a rifle. She reminds me of Joan of Arc and the days of chivalry.[2]

Albert was eventually discharged at Fort Webster on 1 December 1852.[3] From there, Albert and Sarah headed west with the goldseekers en route to California. In 1852 the southern road west led to the Yuma Crossing.

This river crossing to which the Bowmans came is one of the most historic spots in the United States in terms of importance, who passed through, and what occurred there. A fording place near where the Gila and Colorado rivers meet has been used for centuries. Native peoples, conquistadors, missionaries, scalphunters, trappers, soldiers, and settlers have crossed there. Some stayed to live and start businesses, farms, and homes, and gradually a community of sorts was formed.

After the conclusion of the war with Mexico, a boundary commission was created to survey the new boundary between the two countries. The Gila River was to be the main division, but a group led by Lt. Amiel W. Whipple of the Army Corps of Topographical Engineers was sent to the crossing to begin a survey back west to divide Upper and Lower California. On 2 October 1849 they set up camp at the crossing and were besieged by forty-niners who begged for food and directions.[4] They built a ferry to help transport the emigrants across.

The ferry was taken over by Dr. Abel Lincoln, who later was pushed out of business by a gang of cutthroats headed by the notorious scalphunter John Glanton. Glanton abused the Indians and robbed the emigrants who were at his mercy. Finally, the natives could tolerate no more, and on 23 April 1850 they massacred the gang at the crossing. After the story of the slaughter filtered out to California, it was decided that a permanent military presence was necessary at the crossing. In December of 1850 a detachment of men under Lt. Thomas Sweeney pitched tents at what they called Camp Yuma after the tribe there. In March of 1851 they moved, under the guidance of Bvt. Maj. Samuel

Louis J. F. Jaeger ran the ferry at Yuma crossing and was well acquainted with The Great Western. Photo courtesy of Arizona Historical Foundation, Arizona State University Library, Tempe, Arizona.

Heintzelman, to the top of a hill where a permanent facility was to be built. After briefly abandoning the fort due to short supplies and continued Indian troubles, soldiers reoccupied it in February 1852.[5]

Louis J. F. Jaeger had taken over the ferry and was running a successful operation. A true hardheaded frontier businessman, he survived Indian attacks and various disasters to become a fixture at the crossing. During 1850 and 1851, he ferried forty thousand immigrants across the river.[6]

Albert and Sarah would make this remarkable spot their home over the next fourteen years. They would leave on brief forays to other towns in Arizona to seek fortune but would always return to the crossing. Sarah would become acquainted with Heintzelman, Jaeger, and a long list of other notables who passed on the golden road to California. She had seen the beginnings of the gold rush in El Paso and had watched the incredible westward migration over the last two years from New Mexico army camps. She and Albert arrived at this amazing crossroads sometime in December of 1852. The scene that confronted them was full of activity.

The fort had been reestablished on the California side on top of the hill. Jaeger's ferry ran constantly, transporting the endless stream of travelers along with their wagons, thousands of cattle, sheep, and other livestock The Indians, subdued but not above occasional mischief, sold their goods to the travelers and added their own ferry operation.

The biggest problem at the crossing was getting supplies. Food and other essentials had to come hundreds of miles across the desert to the lonely outpost, and the needs of thousands of pioneers constantly stretched the ability of the fort to meet their demands. Sarah and Albert arrived just in time to witness an event that would prove to be the solution to the supply problem.

On 3 September 1852, 120 miles south of the Yuma crossing at the mouth of the Colorado River, the schooner *Capacity* arrived with a cargo of materials for building a steamboat that would be able to float in only twenty-two inches of water. The extreme shallowness of the water and the constantly shifting sand bars had made navigation of the river by a large vessel impossible. When completed, the little steamboat would be called the *Uncle Sam*. The specially designed boat would be sixty five feet long and be powered by a tiny twenty-horsepower engine that turned the sidewheel paddle. It would have a capacity of thirty two tons of freight.[7]

When the *Uncle Sam* arrived at the crossing on 3 December 1852, it must have been an amazing sight, smoking and chugging up to the beach. Second Lt. Thomas W. Sweeney was at the second arrival on Christmas Day 1852 and noted that it took two weeks for the journey between the *Capacity*, anchored at the river's mouth, and the crossing.[8]

Sarah and Albert were present at one of these arrivals. They had traveled there after Albert's discharge on 1 December. They would not have had time to get to the crossing in two days so it must have been the second arrival of the steamboat, on Christmas 1852, that they witnessed. Capt. James Hobbs recalled meeting Sarah at the *Uncle Sam's* arrival.

> At Fort Yuma I met a very large Irish woman called "The Great Western" whom I had seen at Saltillo, when I went there with Colonel Doniphan. She was noted as a camp follower in the Mexican War, was liked universally for her kind motherly ways and, at the battle of Buena Vista, busied herself in making cartridges for the army. I made myself known to her, and she was very glad to see me. She complained that Fort Yuma was the hardest place to secure any fresh supplies that she had ever seen, and begged me to sell her a beef. I sent her one as a present.[9]

The commander of the fort, Maj. Samuel Peter Heintzelman, had been born in 1805 in Pennsylvania. A graduate of West Point in 1826, he had served in Missouri, Michigan, Wisconsin, Florida, and Georgia. He had served in Florida during the Seminole Indian Wars of the 1830s. He was transferred to Buffalo, New York, where he was married and fathered several children.[10] He did not have much chance to enjoy his family, as he was sent to fight in the Mexican War and then was transferred to Yuma. From 1825 through 1872, Heintzelman kept a journal that provides a unique insight into a time of unparalleled westward expansion. At Yuma he proved to be a businessman as well as a military leader. He owned part interest in Jaeger's ferry and became financially involved in many other activities at the crossing.

If, as Hobbs reported, Sarah and Albert were present at the crossing on Christmas 1852, then it is a mystery as to where they spent the next nine months. Heintzelman's first journal entry of their presence is 10 October 1853. In it, they seem to be moving somewhere and have approached him for supplies and help.

"The Great Western called to see me to get some tires reset," he wrote, "I could not refuse when I recollected her services. She was at Fort Brown and 20 years in the Army and once in my company. She looks 50 and is a large, tall, peerless woman."[11]

Sarah was only thirty-nine years old in 1853 and probably would not have appreciated the major's judgment of her appearance, although a hard life on the southwestern frontier undoubtedly aged her. Where they were traveling, or where they had been since Hobbs's sighting of them the previous Christmas, is open to speculation. They probably would not have had been at the crossing all that time without Heintzelman's mentioning them in an earlier entry.

The officers at the fort took notice of her that day during her visit, however, and they "hired the Great Western to keep a mess for them, or rather board them, and she up came after dark, bag and baggage."[12]

Two days later the major noted, "The Western is installed as keeping the mess for Lt. McLean and Bond and the doctor. The others will join when Davidson and O'Connell rturn, if they agree."[13]

Sarah was a promoter. She never missed an opportunity in business and knew the power of advertising. Apparently Heintzelman had shown some animosity or jealousy toward the treatment his officers were receiving from her and must have said or done something that she did not appreciate. He was singled out when "The Western as she calls herself, had a dinner yesterday and everybody in camp but me was invited. She sent to me for butter. I suppose she wanted to show them what she could do in the way of cooking."[14]

Sarah's little promotional gimmick worked. Days later, "The officer's mess par excellent has concluded to join the others and mess with the Western at $20 per month."[15]

Heintzelman refused to join in. Perhaps he felt it beneath his dignity or, as he did not get along very well with many people, he relished his time alone. At any rate, he manufactured a reason for not following along with the others and moving in with the Western, and he found someone to agree with him.

> I had McLean to breakfast with me... McLean is getting tired of the Western's cooking. She does not make as good a breakfast as Hopps [Heintzelman's current cook and landlord] gave us, though it was not as good as usual. Her dinners have fallen off too, the coffee she makes is weak and unsettled.[16]

Albert continued to keep himself employed also. He had a keen interest in mining and never passed up an opportunity to do a little prospecting. The major mentions Albert on several occasions leaving for or returning from various excursions to mining claims in the area.[17]

Heintzelman was constantly dreaming of getting out of the desolate, hot post. He had repeatedly tried to get a replacement, and at last, as the year changed to 1854, he felt a replacement was at hand. He did not know exactly when he would be "set free" but began to sell off any property that he did not want to take with him. Sarah quickly got in her bid. "The Western bought my 4 cows at 60$ each.... I will try to send in some pigs to Eddy to sell for me. I may as well do that or give them away here. The Western wants to buy some but I don't care to ask her what they're worth."[18] Sarah later backed out of her agreement, saying "she will not take my cows, but gave me $20 for my clock."[19]

Something must have occurred at this point that Heintzelman did not clarify. Perhaps he felt, since he was leaving, he did not want to part with bad feelings or realized he had been too hard on her because of his disdain for the place. Whatever the reason, his entries from this date on have a feeling of softening toward her. Gradually they began to develop a relationship.

He decided to give Sarah first choice of his goods for sale. After making an inventory of his property, he and the post sutler, George Hooper, fixed the prices. He noted that "if the Western wants she can have them and if not, I will sell to others."[20] The Major's attitude changed further when he turned on Lieutenant McLean. He had originally counted McLean as an ally when Sarah began to keep the officers' mess, but now "Lt. McLean has fallen out with the Western and left boarding there. He has been very familiar with her and now he puts on dignity. He don't come to my quarters as often as he used to.... I found he was blowing his trumpet too strong on his first arrival." In the same entry he held up Sarah as an example of fairness when he noted "The Western was here today and will take my cows as originally agreed upon. She finds it an excellent bargain."[21]

Heintzelman became more and more supportive of Sarah and began to become critical of anyone who crossed her. McLean quickly became the main target of his current criticism. The major seemed to have resolved his original feelings about Sarah's cooking and he began to dine regularly at her boarding house. On one occasion, "I sent the Western a couple of nice watermelons for our dinner. She gave us a very good dinner, although I hear some of the boarders complain. Some people I would not board. Some people were always late and always complaining."[22]

His feelings for Sarah continued to grow, yet seeing himself as a dignified Major in a sea of insubordinate nonprofessionals, he still felt a need, even in his private writings, to somehow justify his blossoming friendship with a "camp follower."

By 30 January he had made his decision to "join the mess or rather board at Mrs. Bowman's boarding house. I can mess and have a servant for what I pay Hopp and will save my mess bill."[23] The following day he turned over his "furniture and kitchen things to the Western and will commence boarding with her tomorrow."[24]

Once he made the move, things were not perfect, but he was happy.

> Feb. 1, 1854 — I commenced boarding at the Westerns. The breakfast is rather late for me. I get up soon after sunrise and don't have breakfast until 8 o'clock. I have no reason to complain of the meals. She has partially cleaned up my house and it looks very different. I thought Hopps kitchen dirty but she says it is quite clean compared with any of the other messes. She is very well satisfied with the total price of what I let her have. So am I.[25]

When Major Heintzelman moved in, Lieutenant McLean moved out. Later in the same entry, Heintzelman made another dig at McLean while restating his support of Sarah.

Lt. O'Connell has left off boarding with the Western. I suppose from the way McLean has talked. McLean was the one who made the greatest efforts to have her stop here and keep the mess. If things go as they have commenced I will say a good word for her when the Artillery gets out [this refers to his successor's command]... As far as I am personally concerned we are messing pleasantly.[26]

Heintzelman became somewhat possessive of Sarah. His journal entries indicate that he was wrestling with his feelings toward her. When McLean and O'Connell decided to return to boarding at Sarah's place, he noted, "As far as I am concerned I am sorry."[27] The major had little tolerance for either drinking or gambling, and when Sarah told him that Lieutenant Aiken had lost six hundred dollars, he lamented, "I am unfortunate to be connected with drunkards and if gamblers are added, the speculation will soon be under."[28]

On 1 March Major Heintzelman mentioned for the first time the presence of someone from Sarah's past. "The Western and Nancy rode to Pilot Knob and left a Peon woman to cook for us. When they are home it is not much to my taste; but when they are gone it is worse."[29]

"Nancy" was none other than Nancy Skinner, one of the five children shown living with Sarah on the 1850 census in Socorro, New Mexico. They had either been together all along, or had been reunited at the crossing. Heintzelman's next entry seems to indicate that Nancy and Sarah had been together for some time.

Mar. 3, 1854 — The Western is in great trouble. She came to see me about it. Hooper told her there were some people or somebody at S. Diego wants [sic] to take the two orphan girls from her. She took them when they were left destitute and has been a mother to them and is attached to them, and they to her. Nancy, who is now 16, says she will not be taken away from her. She thinks it is Lt. Mason who wants Nancy as a servant to wait on his wife. I should not wonder if it is true. I told her I did not believe it could be him and that I did not think any one could take them from her. She thinks of crossing the river into Sonora with the children. I will afford her every facility for so doing. She has no confidence in Lt. McLean, but thinks him deceitful.[30]

Sarah had appealed to the major and offered her own solution, which was to get out of the country and into Mexico across the river. The name of the second orphan girl is not mentioned. Although Heintzelman gave Nancy's age as sixteen, based on the census her age would be only twelve. Heintzelman bought their story entirely and went about helping them to get away from their pursuers.

Sarah needed a location that would place her home safely in Mexican territory, yet not too far from the fort, as her livelihood depended on the soldiers. The major helped them locate the boundary line and "The Western selected a spot opposite the Fort just within Sonora. Her husband and Nancy are going to live there to avoid this piece of rascality expected from S. Diego. The Western will send all her family over and she with her washerwoman and cook will stay and keep the mess, at least till we go."[31]

Heintzelman's entry indicates that Sarah continued to be a good manager. She had hired others to do the washing and cooking, and she had now ascended to a supervisory role. Albert wasted little time getting started on their new place. The next day the Major "loaned the Western a tent and she sent her people across the river again. Lt. McLean escorted them across."[32]

While Albert worked on the house, Sarah went on with the day-to-day activities of her rapidly expanding business empire. She and the major were continuing a good relationship, although he still found fault with everyone around him. Heintzelman was part owner of the lucrative ferry run by L. J. F. Jaeger at the crossing. Another partner, Capt. William J. Ankrim, had a drinking problem that the major constantly railed against, and George Hooper, post sutler, was also the target of his criticism. Hooper was out rounding up stray cattle on 14 March, and the Major observed in his journal, "Hooper is going to brand them and keep them. The operation is of doubtful morality." He noted Sarah's agreement. "The Western thinks he's very grasping."[33]

Sarah also kept the major abreast of his partner's other dealings. "The Western told me that Hooper had two leagues of land on the river in Lower California. He has it with Mrs. Burton, or rather Burton has it and he is her agent."[34]

Albert had finished the house across the river in Sonora and decided that he also wanted clear title to the land around it, so he hatched a plan to acquire it. Over the years much of the land in northern Mexico had been given to statesmen by the government of Mexico in the form of land grants. Albert and Sarah hoped to purchase one of the grants that included their new home. The major noted in late March that "[Albert] Bowman started yesterday morning for Sonora to try for his [land] grant. Mrs. Bowman tells me there is a merchant in a small town called Magdelena will back them to the extent of $3000. If that is so they can make money."[35]

Sarah now began to set up her business and home across the river. As with any new undertaking, it required quite a bit of her time and the major felt ignored. He complained, "The Western is making a convenience of us. She gives us what she pleases to eat and spends the whole day across the river."[36]

Sarah, the businesswoman, had plans for her new place. It was safe from the jurisdiction of the U. S. Army, yet certainly accessible to the officers and men of the fort, as well as all the travelers who passed through. She had a monopoly and was literally the only game in town. She set up a restaurant, bar, and boarding house. She also got back into the business of supplying women to the soldiers. Heintzelman must have had some inkling as to her plan, although at least in his first entries, he seems truly at a loss. On 1 April he "went to the Western's house. It is going to be a very nice place. I can't see what she expects to do for a living when she moves over there."[37]

He did not have to wait long to find out. The next day the clouds of mystery began to part. A few of the men from the fort went across the river to visit and they "returned drunk. I told the Western it must not occur again."[38]

Sarah did not forget that she needed to stay on the major's good side. She supplied him with favors which he accepted. Her attentions did not go unnoticed by the others at the fort as the major wrote, "I understand the officers are offended because the Western lets her Mexican attend to my mule."[39]

George Hooper noticed the monopoly that Sarah had established across the river and now wanted a piece of the action. He came to Heintzelman to ask his permission to provide a little friendly competition to Sarah, but her friendship was paying off when, on 5 April, the major noted that Hooper was "highly offended because I would not let him build a house on the other side of the river. He says Mr. Bowman's house is on the line but everyone else says it is in Sonora. I have no confidence in him. I would be the best man in camp if I should accede to all his wishes."[40]

The Western was ready to open her new "product line" and realized the need to advertise. Still miffed at the major's favoritism toward Sarah, Hooper turned on her, hoping to gain points with Heintzelman. He decided to keep an eye on her and sent a steady stream of reports to the major. One report apparently roused Heintzelman's puritanical anger and his journal entry refers to Sarah as a "strumpet." He noted that he had "been provoked" at her because she "had a peon come to join her and made the woman swim across the river, or rather she stripped all to her petticoats and got astride a balsa and clasped it with her arms whilst an Indian pushed her across. It must have been an interesting sight."[41]

Another event of interest was about to occur — Nancy's birthday. This would be, according to the census, her thirteenth birthday or, according to Heintzelman, her seventeenth. The major donated to the merriment of the celebration when he "gave the Western an order for a couple of bottles of champaign [sic] to take across the river for Nancy's birthday."[42]

Nancy certainly seemed to feel she had achieved womanhood as she quickly moved on to the next step. Six days later on 19 April, "The Western came and asked if I would not care to witness the marriage of her orphan girl (Nancy) to Burke, a sergeant discharged from a company in New Mexico. It is to take place tomorrow night in camp and then cross the river." Nancy apparently had a choice of suitors, as Heintzelman added: "She had three more strings to her bow and this, I think is by far the best one."[43]

The next night was the big event. Everyone from the fort attended and Heintzelman filed a full report of the evening's activities in his diary.

> Quite an unusual event took place last night. Burke was married to Nancy Skinner the Western's adopted daughter. It took place in McLeans and O'Connells quarters. McLean repeated a long ceremony and Squire Jaeger stood by to legalize it. [Jaeger, was also the justice of the peace.][44] [Albert] Bowman got back yesterday morning from Sonora [with his grant]. I first intended not to go as it was in McLean's quarters, but his conduct was so different at tea, I thought it would be better. After tattoo, the Ethiopian Band came in and we had dancing, songs and recitations. Two of the women from under the hill [prostitutes] were there and in that way we made up a set. So few of the gentlemen dance, I had to

make one of the sets. We had supper and I did not leave till near 2 a.m. I believe it was three before it broke up. The officers gave more liquor to some of the men who came into a side room and they got drunk. Some rather misbehaved last night.[45]

The wedding of Nancy to Sergeant Burke and the subsequent reception was a resounding success. All agreed that it had been a fine celebration, and Sarah was able to gain some business as well. The soldiers now knew where to go for all of their "needs." Everyone had such a good time in fact, that they all went back over the next night. Heintzelman joined the others, but still tried to maintain his distance. He felt he needed to justify the appropriateness of his being there, even to himself in his diary.

> April 22, 1854 — I modified the order about officers gone from the post. I allow them to cross to the Westerns' in a small boat during the day; but when they wish to take another boat, or go at night, they must ask. We all but the officer of the Day went across with the band and staid [sic] till near 12 o'clock. The Western wished to take them two women but I objected. It was bad enough to ask them the night before. [He is referring to "the women from under the hill." Due to a shortage of women at the crossing, Sarah tried to supply dance partners for the party.] She has a nice house. I was very sorry I agreed to go but when you are in Rome you must do as Rome does. I have not surrendered the principal [sic] on which I acted with regard to the officers but the modification has satisfied them.[46]

George Hooper's memory of the night must have been clouded by a little too much to drink, and Sarah teased him about it by telling him how he had acted. Heintzelman adds that "Hooper called and apologized for his conduct before he left. He heard some stories from the Western he at first believed."[47]

Sarah's place had become the center of attraction at the fort. The officers continued their daily visits, and the next afternoon "we all went across the river...on the Westerns invitation it helped pass the day."[48] Heintzelman was aware that he must maintain his professional image and not appear too eager, so he restrained himself from accepting every invitation. A week later he wrote, "The officers have gone over the river to the Westerns to an oyster supper given by themselves I believe. The Western wanted me to go but I could not on her invitation."[49]

He continued his personal battle against the presence of liquor and recorded one day that Sarah "has an Englishman of the name of Spence who has brought a few things to sell. Liquor I presume will be the principal article of trade." The Western realized that she needed to continue to keep the Major as an ally, and she "sent me a piece of Petahia' [sic]. It is a species of cactus, columnar. It is in the form of seeds cemented together by a sweet reddish substance. Tolerably palatable."[50]

Sarah seemed to know just how to manipulate the major and keep him happy, as within a week he was back at her door. 9 May was "the anniversary of the Battle of Resaca de la Palma [in the Mexican War] and I had the officers at my quarters to have a drink. After dinner we took a small boat and rowed across the river and called at the Westerns."[51]

By the end of May 1854, Heintzelman knew he was close to leaving the fort. He heard that Brevet Major Thomas was due to arrive by boat in San Diego soon and would proceed from there to Fort Yuma to relieve him of his despised duty. He began to prepare to leave in earnest. As furniture and supplies were hard to find at such a lonely outpost, he had a ready market for any goods that he did not want to take with him. Sarah was entering the business of dealing in used furniture. She saw the keen market at the fort and used her friendship with the major to get first bid in on his things, with the intent of reselling them to soldiers or travelers at a profit. The major and Sarah did not always see eye to eye on all of the transactions. One day Heintzelman presented Sarah with a bill of what she had purchased. She complained of the total so he explained that, "she need not take anything she does not want or thought too high and I would take back what she had not used." Heintzelman had sold her nearly one third of the items he had for sale. He had considered giving her some of the things for nothing, but worried that she would tell the others of her special treatment. He felt his prices were more than fair and wrote that "California prices would not suit her. She begged me for everything she saw, whether I wished to sell it or not and now complains of the total amount."[52]

Sarah continued to try Heintzelman's patience, yet even when she broke the rules, he did not blame her. When one of the men got drunk, he concluded that it was "no doubt, from the liquor McLean gave the Western an order to get from the sutlers although he knew it contrary to my orders." He demanded that McLean not violate his orders again, or he would prohibit the sutler from selling liquor at all. McLean's insubordination left the major disgusted, and he added, "I never saw a more unreasonable man."[53]

In June Sarah once again irritated the major by hedging on an agreement. Her business across the river was continuing to increase and she needed some extra help, so she pulled one of her workers from the fort. Sarah had "agreed to let her boy water and feed my mule and yesterday told me I must get someone to do it, as she had sent her boy across the river. A cool way of getting out of her engagement." Apparently he was quite miffed and added, "As soon as the troops arrive I will change my eating place." He also managed to get in another jab at McLean when he noted that the Lieutenant had done something "without consulting anyone but her, at least so far as I know. She does just what she pleases with him."[54]

Heintzelman backed off on his threat to go somewhere else for his meals, and a week later Sarah sent him a peace offering. "I was down on board the steamer boat this forenoon and when I got home I found a pitcher of very fine [unreadable] the Western had sent me."[55]

Heintzelman continued to single out McLean for criticism and blamed him for an ongoing problem at the fort, while once again allying himself with the Western. "We had a good deal of trouble about the time for our meals and at last McLean had to conform for the time and go by that of the garrison. I suspect he finds he gains nothing by kicking. Even the Western is tired of his caprices. They quarrel like two young lovers."[56]

The replacements at last arrived, and an elated Heintzelman prepared to depart the scorching desert. It was time to settle up with Sarah. He owed her money for boarding with her and she owed him for goods he had sold her. On 8 July, after working out his version of the balance, "I sent for the Western and pointed out the balance of my things and have struck a balance she still owes me $155 — the total amount was $238.60."[57]

Sarah was willing to pay up, but a week later brought along a bill of her own. The major was less than satisfied and angrily commented,

"She could not offer me any inducement to live again as I have done the last 6 months. Her bill for 14 days is over 97 dollars — twice as much as necessary." He felt sorry for the new arrivals since they had "come unprovided for messing and have to fall in with her." He took one parting shot at Lieutenant McLean. The Western's bill may have been excessive but, "Lt. McLean does just as she says and he signed her books."[58]

The next day Major Heintzelman left Yuma and Sarah.

CHAPTER 5

Arizona Travels

On 30 June 1854 the United States formalized the sale of land by Mexico known as the Gadsden Purchase. The sale had been agreed to on 30 December 1853, but was held up by Congress until the June date.[1] The United States did not take formal possession of its new property until 1856 when it sent soldiers into the area to set up posts in Tucson and Calabasas.[2] Some entrepreneurs quickly noted that there was a profit to be made by making a purchase in the new area before too many people arrived.

On 11 July 1854 Heintzelman noted that two surveyors, Charles Poston and Herman Ehrenberg, had arrived. "They want to lay out a town here and are backed by capitalists in S. Francisco. They propose an arrangement with Ankrim and Jaeger for a town near the Ferry, or rather to include it."[3] These two men were schemers who had hatched a complex plan to purchase some land they thought the railroad would need in the newly acquired territory. They hoped to buy the land, quietly wait and then sell it to the railroad at a greatly inflated price. The problem was that they did not know the exact route the railroad would take, and the two went through a stream of bad luck trying to find it. Eventually, they arrived at the Yuma crossing and determined that the area near the Fort would be where the railroad would pass on its way to San Diego.

Seven years later, in 1861, Poston was traveling with a friend, geologist Raphael Pumpelly. The two were fleeing the bandits and Indians that were ransacking southern Arizona since federal troops had been withdrawn due to the Civil War. As they neared the crossing,

Arizona pioneer Charles Poston, who met Sarah at Yuma crossing. Photo courtesy of Arizona Department of Library, Archives and Public Records.

Poston told Pumpelly a story about the survey that he and Ehrenberg had made that day in 1854.

Poston claimed that they had arrived at the river completely broke and could not afford the twenty-five-dollar ferry charge from Jaeger to cross the river. He and Ehrenberg decided on a little ploy to get a free trip across. They set up their survey equipment and began to lay out stakes and make up maps, as though they were creating town lots and waterfront property. Louis Jaeger quietly watched from across the river and finally let his curiosity lead him across. He asked what they were doing and was told by Poston that they were laying out lots for what would become a great city called Colorado City. With grand gestures and eloquent exaggerations, he convinced Jaeger that he was serious. Jaeger excitedly asked how much a lot would cost and Poston quoted him twenty five dollars, which was, coincidentally, the same price as their ferriage. Jaeger eagerly gave passage to the party in return for the deed to his new property. The 936 acres Poston laid out as Colorado City were registered in California at San Diego.[4] Heintzelman and Ankrim were among those listed as owners of lots.

George Hooper was also one of those who bought lots in the new city, and now he looked to expand his business operations over to the new territory. As Heintzelman had left, Hooper wasted little time in making his move and Sarah provided an easy way to get started by renting out her house to him. He moved his store into it, and Sarah and Albert moved back across the river to the the fort.

An article in the *Arizona Sentinel* on 25 August 1877 stated that the building was "the first regular house in Yuma" and gives the location as the "southwest corner of Main and First streets." It mentions that Hooper "and Dr. George McKinstry, who had come out as sutlers for the troops, occupied her house as a store."

Soon the "Bowman building" was not big enough, and the firm moved to a new site down near the steamboat landing. Hooper filed an affidavit on 14 July 1865, ten years later, claiming to have bought the land from Albert and Sarah. He stated that, "during the year A. D. 1853 or 1854," he bought the land that Albert had gotten in the grant. He paid fifteen hundred dollars for it and said that Albert gave him a deed to the property. Albert, according to Hooper, had gotten the grant from the prefect of San Ygnacio in 1853, and the papers were kept in the house. Hooper stated that the house burned down in 1854 and the deed and grant were destroyed.[5] Hooper was seeking to establish his rightful ownership by giving the affidavit.

On 14 December 1865 Albert gave his statement to the justice of the peace, Frank Hewitt. He stated that he got the grant in April 1853 and corroborates the 1854 date of sale and the amount of the transaction. Albert and Sarah agreed that they gave the papers to Hooper, but they said that they were swept away in "the Great Flood of the Gila River, January 22, A. D. 1862."[6] This version seems more likely as far as dates are concerned, as the house is reported to have been there until at least 1861. Further, as the Bowmans moved back and forth to the fort over the next few years, it would seem that Hooper may have bought the land, but not necessarily the house.

Sarah and Albert continued to capitalize on the activity around the crossing. As the stream of humanity continued to pass through, the fort was being enlarged and needed building supplies. Albert and Sarah made an agreement on 12 October 1854 with 1st Lt. Beckman DuBarry, the acting assistant quartermaster, to supply adobe bricks for construction of public buildings. They were to produce 700,000 adobes "fifteen inches in length, ten inches in breadth, and four inches in thickness." A contract was drawn up which stipulated that they would receive fifteen dollars per thousand bricks or $10,500 total for the job. Because the project would take a little time to accomplish, the parties agreed that payment would be made monthly, based on the number of bricks produced. This contract is one of the few documents that show Sarah's "X." As she could neither read nor write, Albert signed for her, and she placed "her mark," as it was designated.[7]

Albert, in addition, found work as a laborer for two dollars a day with the quartermaster.[8] Apparently he and Sarah continued to get along with the new management at the fort as well as they had with Heintzelman. With Sarah back at work at the officers' mess and with Albert making adobes, working as a laborer, and mining, they were quite productive.

Bvt. Maj. George Henry Thomas had taken over as commander of

Sylvester Mowry who served at Fort Yuma and referred to Sarah as "an admirable pimp." Photo courtesy of Arizona Historical Foundation, Arizona State University Library, Tempe, Arizona.

the fort from Heintzelman on 15 July 1854 and would stay only a year until 21 July 1855. He continued the construction begun by Heintzelman and had a mule-powered pump installed to raise water seventy feet up to a reservoir at the fort. He also had new rifles suppled to the men and, overall, served his year quietly by improving the conditions at Fort Yuma.[9]

Bvt. Lt. Col. Martin Burke assumed command on 21 July 1855. The following month 1st Lt. Sylvester Mowry arrived at the fort. Mowry was a flamboyant frontier character who was obsessed with the opposite sex. With the help of his superiors, he had fled Utah a year earlier after attempting to seduce Mary Young, daughter-in-law of Brigham Young. After being reassigned to California, he arrived at Fort Yuma on 28 August 1855.[10]

He hated the desert, where he was out of the mainstream of life and unable to experience the pleasures he had become accustomed to. On 29 October 1855 he wrote to his friend Edward J. Bicknall in Providence, Rhode Island, and complained of the heat and isolation as well as the lack of amusement.[11]

The hot-blooded lieutenant was eventually able to locate a seventeen year old Mexican girl to provide him with some companionship and he described her to Bicknall. Mowry then indicated that "she is living with the 'Great Western' and comes up nights to my room."[12]

As a postscript, he added a brief biography of his supplier, noting her record with the army and adding that "Among her other good qualities she is an admirable 'pimp'. She used to be a splendid looking woman and has done 'good service' — but is too old for that now."[13]

Mowry would go on to become commander at Fort Yuma in 1857 and continued his womanizing there up to his discharge in 1858. He would work for the creation of a separate territory for Arizona and have a wildly fluctuating financial history, due primarily to an incident that occurred during the Civil War. His mine, developed after his discharge, was confiscated by Union forces when he was accused of having Confederate ties. The accusations were false, yet he was held in the guardhouse at Yuma pending an investigation. By the time he was released, his mine had been looted and his equipment destroyed. He tried vainly to get retribution from the government and, though he did recover ownership of the mine, he was never able to recover financially. He died a pauper in England in 1871 of a kidney disease.[14]

The diary of L. J. F. Jaeger, the ferry operator, was lost for forty years until a trunk was found in a ditch near a house that he had owned. Inside were a few pages of his journal. He was connected with the crossing from 1850 to 1877, but the only surviving pages are from 11 December 1855 to 2 July 1857. Jaeger was mostly concerned with his personal business and only casually mentioned historic figures or events as sidelights. A few of the fragments mention Sarah.[15]

The first is 17 December 1855, when he described Sarah paying off a debt. "Westron [sic] sent down $100 dollars on the old account and $20 on the new account."[16] On 21 March 1856, Jaeger, in his typical understatement, casually mentions the end of an odyssey which was to electrify and fascinate the curious public for years to come — the five-year captivity of Olive Oatman by Indians. Her surviving brother Lorenzo had come to be re-united with her at the fort. Jaeger wrote in his awkward style: "We had a warm day, and Oatman got in [Lorenzo] from Los Angeles also after his sister also, and I went up to the Fort with him also, and she did not know him and he did not know her also, so much change in 5 years."[17]

The saga of Olive Oatman was the stuff of soap opera and would eventually end with her meeting The Great Western. Royce Oatman, his wife Mary, and their seven children had traveled from Fulton, Illinois, through Independence, Missouri, then followed the Santa Fe trail west. They got as far as a spot about eighty miles east of Fort Yuma following Cooke's wagon road along the Gila River. After spending most of the day pushing, pulling, and dragging their wagon, horses, and supplies up to the top, they collapsed in exhaustion and prepared a meager evening meal. At sunset a group of Indians, probably Yavapai, approached and asked for food. When they did not receive enough, they attacked the family with clubs and killed the mother, father, and four of the children outright. The oldest son, Lorenzo, about fourteen years old, was struck down and thrown over the edge of the mesa and left for dead. Olive, age thirteen, and Mary Ann, age seven, were taken off to captivity. Over the next five years they would be sold to the Mohaves, Mary Ann would die of starvation, and Olive would resign herself to a life of captivity.

Olive Oatman, who was cared for by The Great Western at Yuma after five years of Indian captivity. Photo courtesy of Arizona Department of Library, Archives and Public Records.

Meanwhile, Lorenzo had crawled back to civilization, recovered from his wounds, and spent the five years searching for his sisters. Finally, in February of 1856, a Yuma Indian named Francisco told Henry Grinnell, a carpenter at the fort, that he knew the Mohaves had Olive and that he could get her back. Grinnell worked with Post Commander Burke and sent a ransom of beads, blankets, and a horse with Francisco, who bartered for her release.[18]

She arrived at the fort on 22 February 1856 and was placed under the charge of Sarah until her brother Lorenzo could come to meet her. Charles Poston described the story of the massacre and captivity, then added, "Captain Grenelle [sic] and party had but little difficulty in bartering for Olive, and brought her to Yuma where she was placed in the charge of the 'Great Western', who then kept a mess table at Yuma."[19]

Edward Tuttle served at Fort Yuma as a lieutenant and many years later, in the 1920s, recalled his experiences in a series of letters. In one, he refers to the return of Olive Oatman. Her escort "delivered her at Fort Yuma and she was cared for by a woman known as the Great Western and finally sent to an uncle in California."[20]

Olive told her story to the Reverend Royal B. Stratton, who wrote a highly dramatized book called *The Captivity of the Oatman Girls*. She spoke of her experiences to various groups to promote the book and to raise money for church groups. She met and married John Fairchild, a successful businessman, and eventually died at age sixty-five on 20 March 1903.[21]

The next mention of Sarah comes again from Jaeger, who mentions on four occasions in his diary her having a serious illness for three weeks in early summer 1856.[22]

Sarah was fully recovered in October of 1856, as she traveled with Soloman Warner, an early pioneer, from Yuma to Tucson along with several others. She and Albert were expanding their business interests. They packed their goods and some of their employees and made their move to central Arizona. She had obviously become somewhat attached to Olive Oatman, as the group made a stop at the massacre site, according to Warner.

> George Hooper, Willium [sic] Thompson and The Great Westerny [sic] accompanied me back. This party buried the bones of the Oatman family. The bones were taken from the top of the hill. They were in a pile of rocks with some broken

crockery. They were taken down into the bottom and buried near the road. On the north side of the road. The most the work was don [sic] by the peones of the Great Western.[23]

Albert and Sarah bought lot twenty-one in Tucson on 28 October 1856 from Frederick A. Ronstadt.[24] The purpose was apparently to test the waters of Tucson for financial possibilities. For a time they took boarders, one of whom, John G. Capron, gave an affidavit used for Albert's pension records on 15 December 1897. He stated that "In the fall of 1856, I boarded with Albert Bowman and Sarah his wife at Tucson, Arizona, and was ever well acquainted with them both."[25]

After acquiring the Gadsden Purchase, the United States needed to send troops to establish a presence and formally take possession of this newest property. Sarah wanted to be near the soldiers, so when Camp Moore was established by the dragoons in late 1856 at Calabasas Ranch in southern Arizona by the Santa Cruz river, she began to contemplate moving. When Maj. Enoch Steen was ordered to locate a spot nearer to Tucson the following spring, he established Fort Buchanan along the head of Sonoita Creek.[26] That was enough draw for Sarah, and she and Albert quickly sold their boarding house property in Tucson to Richard M. Doss on 29 January 1857 and moved south to be near the new fort.[27]

Jeff Ake met the Western when he was about ten years old. He lived with his father, Felix Ake, who had a ranch near the fort. In his recollections, he described Sarah and her saloon at Patagonia. "She packed two six-shooters, and they all said she shore could use 'em, that she had killed a couple of men in her time." She bought eggs from Jeff and told him "there was just one thin sheet of sandpaper between Yuma and Hell."[28]

Her place had been quite a popular "resort," according to Solomon Warner. It also got a little rough, and no doubt Sarah put her six-shooters to work on occasion. Warner related several killings around Tucson during the period including two at Sarah's saloon. He recalled, "the next killing was don [sic] tin [sic] miles below ... on the Sonoita at the house of Mrs. Bowman, better known by the name of the Great Western by army officers. There were two Mexicans killed by the Americans at a dance."[29]

Sarah was thriving in her new location, proving again her ability to move into an area and develop a successful business. Whatever was needed, she provided. No record exists of what Albert was doing during this period, but he probably worked around the fort and did odd jobs.

In late 1858 attention was focused back toward the Yuma crossing when gold was discovered twenty miles up the Gila River from the fort. Arizona was about to experience its first gold rush. Gold fever produced a town of 1,200 "future millionaires."[30] Gila City sprang from the desert into a bustling place filled with miners and those who made their living from the miners.

All of this excitement was not ignored by Albert and Sarah. At least one source indicated that they intended to get into the boom-town business. The *San Joaquin Republican* of Stockton, California, on 15 December 1858 reported the following:

> THE GILA: — Mr. Ordeman of San Francisco informs the *National* of that city, that Gila City, (in the mines) has been surveyed by him. Lots have been sold on main street 25 by 80 feet, for around 25$ to 50$. Several houses have been built, and Mr. Bowman will soon commence his erection of a hotel which will be kept by the "Great Western".

The mines played out in 1861. Albert and Sarah, as far is known, never set up any business in Gila City, and within a few weeks the town was deserted.

The Bowmans returned to the crossing in 1860. As they are later noted back at the Sonoita Creek location a year later, they were likely either visiting Yuma when the census taker showed up on 8 October 1860, or were able somehow to maintain businesses in both places from that time on.[31] The census lists them together. Albert gave his age as thirty-two and Sarah showed hers to be forty-seven. Albert listed his profession as "upholsterer." Sarah gave no profession, despite the fact that she had consistently demonstrated a keen business ability and started several kinds of businesses across the Southwest. She gave her value of real estate as "$2,000" and Albert's as "$600," which seems to prove again her skill at making money, as well as demonstrating that she intended to keep her own money. Her birthplace is listed as "Tennessee" and Albert's as "Brunswick, Germany." Sarah is noted again as being unable to read or write. Three others are shown to be living with them: Lucia Lopez, age fifteen, from Mexico; Henry Lopez, age two, from New Mexico; and Jose Maria, age fifteen, an "Indian" from New Mexico. No occupation or real estate value is listed for them. Interestingly, the census taker made footnotes for Albert, Sarah, and Lucia at the bottom of the page.

Albert's note reads: "Mr. Bowman was born, Mrs. B thinks in Brunswick, Gy." This seems to indicate that Albert was not there to answer for himself. Sarah's note reads: "Mrs. Bowman is the 'Heroine of Fort Brown' and the 'Great Western' of Mexican War celebrity." Lucia's footnote indicates that she "was quite young for a mother at the birth of her first child." Assuming her age to be accurate, she would have been thirteen when Henry was born. No mention is made of Nancy Skinner Burke or her unnamed sister, who were noted six years earlier by Heintzelman, so Sarah had taken in three new charges. She may have employed them at one of her various enterprises, or perhaps they were simply boarders.

As 1861 arrived, so too came rumblings from the east. Tensions were accelerating toward what seemed an inevitable conflict between the north and the south. When hostilities finally commenced, the north was forced to pull its troops from isolated Arizona to help protect its other fronts and to conserve funds. The protection of citizens from Apaches and the presence of the military as a deterrent to bandits on the southwestern frontier were of secondary importance to a government struggling to survive. The pioneers would simply have to fend for themselves.

The Indians watched with interest as federal troops were withdrawn. They thought that the whites were at last surrendering and going back to where they had come from. They interpreted the soldiers' actions as meaning that they could have their land back and went on a rampage against any citizens who remained. For a time, lawlessness ruled in the Southwest.

Jeff Ake was present on 21 July 1861 when the troops abandoned Fort Buchanan. They withdrew and burned what was left so the Indians and any Confederates who might come by would gain nothing from the remains. According to Ake, the troops gave the civilians three days notice of their departure and told them they could have any supplies the soldiers left behind. "The Great Western, 'The greatest whore in the West' my Dad called her... sent her girls back to Mexico where they come from."[32]

The wagon train moved east toward New Mexico, but Sarah and Albert only went with it as far as Tucson, then turned west toward the crossing. Like most others in the area, they withdrew from the unprotected central Arizona section and went to the crossing where the fort was maintained through the war. The southern route appealed to the Confederates as a way to move into, and capture, California. The Yankees were aware of the importance of the spot, and vowed to hold it.

With the Apaches on fresh waves of murdering and looting, and bandits taking advantage of the absence of law, Tucson became a walled refuge. Likewise, it was a virtual prison for its inhabitants, as they could not venture beyond those protective walls without risking their lives. Two travelers who were moving away from the chaos of central Arizona in 1861 were Raphael Pumpelly and Charles Poston. As they fled toward the crossing, Poston told Pumpelly his story about surveying Colorado City in a ruse to get free ferriage across the river seven years earlier. After hearing it, Pumpelly was eager to see what had become of the "city." They arrived at Sarah's house that morning and, pausing outside, Pumpelly recounted the following exchange:

> "How about the city?" I asked Poston. "There it is; we'll breakfast in it", he answered, pointing to the miserable house. And we did; and in breakfasting, with the exception of the proprietress, our party formed the entire population of a city eight years old.
>
> Our landlady, known as the "Great Western," no longer young, was a character of a varied past. She had followed our army throughout the war of 1848 with Mexico. Her relations with the soldiers were of two kinds. One of these does not admit of analysis; the other was angelic, for she was adored by the soldiers for her bravery in the field and for her unceasing kindness in nursing the sick and wounded.
>
> Having heard her history from Poston, I looked with interest on this woman as, with quiet native dignity, she served our simple meal. She was a lesson in the complexity of human nature.[33]

The Confederates hoped to quickly grab New Mexico and Arizona and then advance on to California. Capt. Sherrod Hunter occupied Tucson for the Confederacy on 28 February 1862.[34] Residents of the besieged town had welcomed his troops without firing a shot. The promise of protection from the Indians by soldiers, no matter which side they were on, was enough for them. Most residents quickly swore allegiance to the Confederacy. Hunter had heard that the North was sending a column of volunteers toward Arizona to secure the route, so he resolved to destroy any supplies that might have any value to the advancing Yankees.

The volunteers coming from the west were headed by Col. James Henry Carleton and were made up of 1,600 men known as the California Column. Lt. Col. J. R. West had been sent ahead of the column to secure supplies, and the main body arrived at Fort Yuma on 16 February 1862.[35] With them was George H. Pettis, who wrote: "The command arrived at Fort Yuma and went into camp. Here we met Don Pascual, head chief of the Yuma, Don Diego Jaeger and 'The Great Western', three of the most celebrated characters in the annals of Fort Yuma."[36]

The California Column moved east. A skirmish at Picacho Peak, between an advance Union detachment headed by Lt. James Barrett and a small rebel force on 15 April 1862, resulted in the deaths of Lieutenant Barrett and two other Union soldiers and left four wounded. The Confederates suffered one killed, four wounded, and three taken prisoner. This has been called the westernmost battle of the Civil War. Confederate Captain Hunter in Tucson had heard that his comrades in New Mexico had not fared too well. Under leadership of Henry Hopkins Sibley, the rebels had encountered defeat at Glorieta Pass and were in retreat. Faced with no reinforcements to his rear and an advancing California Column in front of him, Captain Hunter abandoned Tucson on 4 May 1862. It was soon reoccupied by Union forces.[37]

Except for troop movements passing through, Fort Yuma would have little to do with the remaining part of the Civil War. Sarah continued to run her various businesses, relatively uninterrupted by the violence of the war across the continent. If anything, the fresh troops arriving were a new source of income for her. Lt. Edward D. Tuttle arrived in February 1863. One of the first people he met at the Fort was Sarah.

> At the time of arrival at the Fort, Feb, 1863, as I was sitting in front of my room trying to eliminate some of the dust acquired during my 300 miles tramp; I was accosted by a large American woman, a six footer, and proportionately broad with: "Lieutenant have you any washing you want done?" I hastened to hand her the only change of shirts I

had. I enquired who she was and was informed she was the best known woman in the American Army..."The Great Western."

He goes on to give a brief mention of her history in the war and adds:

> She had adopted three Mexican children and raised them (one boy and two girls) to maturity; the boy a fine cook; the girls helpers in her Laundry. She was a splendid example of the American frontier woman.[38]

Tuttle is also the source for another story: "She had an order for a ration for life.... She was assigned to my company 'H' 4th Inf. for drawing her rations and rated a Co. Laundress."[39] The reference to Sarah's being given a "ration for life" is repeated several times in his letters but is unsubstantiated by documentation.

On 24 February 1863 Arizona became a separate territory and in 1864 a special territorial census was taken. It showed Albert as the only Bowman living in Arizona City. It gave his age as thirty-five and his occupation as miner.[40] The various record books of the mines and claims around Yuma are liberally sprinkled with Albert's name. He was owner or part owner of dozens of claims and mines with varying degrees of success.[41]

The census also indicates that Albert is single. Sarah is not seen on the census, which is understandable, as she was working primarily across the river at the fort in California. Albert's and Sarah's separate careers had pulled them apart. Working as a laundress, cook, and landlady at the fort necessitated her being there all the time. She was fifty-one years old in 1864. Pumpelly had described her three years earlier as "no longer young." Her life of hardship on the southwest frontier was beginning to wear on her. Sarah was looking for security at this stage of her life. She was gainfully employed, respected by the soldiers, officers, and others, and lived in relative comfort.

Albert, on the other hand, was only thirty-six. He was madly seeking his fame and fortune in the hills of southwestern Arizona. He had done his time as a soldier and, other than the security offered by their presence, he had no particular need for the military. Hardrock mining was a demanding, lonely job. Endless days spent scrambling across rocky slopes, searching for telltale glimmers of gold, or hammering into hard packed desert earth were the lot of a miner. Like Sarah, his work required long weeks or months spent out on the job with little time for a wife. The two had simply grown apart.

The fort had some problems of its own in 1864. The two biggest disciplinary problems for the army of the frontier were disertion and theft. Hard work, low pay, intolerable heat, bad food, and loneliness contributed to Fort Yuma's desertion rate. Frequently, deserters left with government property. Guns, horses, saddles, and other supplies could be sold to civilians eager to have the latest firearms or hard-to-find materials. Often soldiers and officers at distant outposts gave in to temptation and sold government property to the townspeople. The army supplies were sorely needed by everyone in the area, and a considerable profit could be realized for scarce goods. From 1862 through 1863, a somewhat open sale of army supplies went on uncontrolled. It was eventually discovered, and depositions were taken in an effort to bring the guilty persons to justice.

Sarah had been there throughout the period, so naturally she was asked for her story. The subsequent affidavit is possibly the only official statement that she ever gave that has survived. Taken on 25 July 1864 by Lt. J. M. Starkweather, post adjutant, the first sentence reveals yet another occupation that Sarah held at Fort Yuma.

> I have been Hospital Matron, at Fort Yuma, for 11 years, — I know Col. Bowie, of the 5th Cal. Inf. In the Summer of 1862, while he was in Command of this Post, I went to him and requested permission to build a Corral for my sheep, on the reserve. He told me, that I might as well turn them into the "Grave Yard" for they would clean it out — it was at that time, over grown with weeds.
>
> Upon this permission I put the Sheep (about 50 in numbers) into the "Grave Yard" and they remained there, until they were all killed for eating at the rate of two or three a week. They remained until after Col. Bowie relinquished the Command to Capt. Thayer and during most of the time, the latter was in Command, the yard was used as a Corral for the Sheep. They were shut up in it at night and turned out in the day time.
>
> The "Grave Yard" was left all this time in very bad condition, the "Graves" were trampled down and the fence was down. It remained in this condition until Major Bennett took command of the Post in Sept. 1863. It was then fixed up by

him. I think the Sheep did some good by eating down the weeds.

Question: State what you know about the Sale of Govt. Stores at Fort Yuma during the years of 1862 and 1863.

Ans: Soon after Capt. Thayer took Command he loaded six to eight Mules out of the Commissary with Sugar, Flour, Bostons, Molasses and Tea.

He also told me that whenever I saw miners who wanted provisions to send them to him, that he had some to sell. This was kept up during all the time he was in Command and continued by Capt. French. Capt. Thayer also sold the rations of Dr. Cox and other Officers. At that time Commissary stores sold here for large prices in gold.

It was a common thing at this time to see Mules taking Provisions away from this Post. I have often had miners enquire of me where they could get 'Grub' and used to send them to Capt. Thayer. He also told me to sell all my surplus Provisions.

One night I was in Dr. Woosters Quarters. Dr. Wooster, his wife, Lieut. Lambert [unreadable] and Capt. Thayer were there. We were playing 'Euchre'. Capt. Thayer said to Mrs. Wooster, 'Madame I have made a good sale to day' — at the same time he drew out a purse containing at least $100 Dolls. in Gold Dust, and a pair of earrings which he said he paid $18 Dolls. for. During the time Capt. Thayer was in Command Dr. Wooster, at the time Surgeon here, drew from the Commissary Stores, and sold as much as 1300 lbs. of Potatoes. They were packed away openly from the rear of the Officers Quarters.

Capt. Thayer also drew from the Commissary large amounts of Potatoes and sold them in the same way. At this time I as Hospital Matron, could not get a potato to eat, Capt. Thayer saying he could not let me have any. At this time Potatoes were 75 Cts. per 100 lbs. and could be Sold for $12.50 Dolls. per 100 lbs. in Gold.

One day Sergt. Jones, Orderly Sergt. of Co. 'C. 5th Cal. Inst. came into my Quarters and threw down a purse of $40 in Gold, saying why don't you all have money like I do? I said I don't know how you get money. He replied — Capt. Thayer allows me to sell Flour, out of the Commissary. I buy for $4 Dolls. and sell for $10 Dolls. It was almost an every day thing to see Mules, and 'burrows' packing Flour away from the Post during this time. Sergt. Parker Co. 'H' 5 Cal. Infry. at that time Commissary Sergt. must know many facts.

her
Sarah X Bowman
mark[42]

Col. G. W. Bowie, who Sarah had said allowed her to graze her sheep in the cemetery, got a chance to reply to the charges that were leveled by Sarah and others against him of sale of government stores. He denied all of the charges and addressed, in his statement, the issue of the cemetery being used as a corral. He wrote:

> As for making a sheep-pen of the cemetery I know nothing, for there were not a dozen sheep at Yuma, all of the time I was there. Mrs. Bowman bought a few head for her mess which probably lasted two weeks, and I do not really recollect whether I gave her permission to put them in there at night or not. I do know she had no such permission in the day time, and she will tell you that they strayed away several times.[43]

It seems that little in the way of punishment actually occurred, due primarily to the parties involved either being dead or discharged and some conflicting testimony being given. When asked, however, Sarah had done her duty and testified as to what she knew for the investigators. She continued in her business at the fort through 1864-1865. The only activity traceable to her in 1865 is the trading of affidavits mentioned earlier with George Hooper concerning ownership of the land Albert had gotten across the river. The house had washed away in the flood of 1862, but the town was slowly rebuilding. Albert continued to file claims to mines throughout 1865 and was elected chairman of the silver mining district at a meeting 1 March 1865.[44] There is no way to tell how well his claims panned out, but he was becoming a respected member of the mining community in the area. He had found his niche for a time and also found something else.

On the census of April 1866, a special U.S. census done in Arizona, Albert is listed as head of family.[45] Directly beneath his name, is listed

Mary A. Bowman. Mary Jane Bailey had assumed his last name. Albert had found some time between mining excursions to start a new relationship that would last the rest of his life.

Most of the information available about Mary is confined to the applications that she later filled out for a widow's pension after Albert's death. The records indicate that they were not married until 9 December 1868, by a justice of the peace in Yuma. Mary referred to Sarah as "Sarah Knight" several times on the application. "Knight" may be a mistake, or perhaps, a clue to Sarah's maiden name. Mary gave her own birthdate as 6 November 1844, "near Nashville, Tenn.," which would make her only twenty-one in April 1866, to Albert's thirty-eight. She also gave this somewhat bland description of Albert on the application: "Complexion- dark. Eyes- dark. Hair- dark." His occupation is listed as "Ferryman" on one form and "upholsterer" on another.[46]

Sarah was listed on another page of the same census and was shown to be living with her old friend Lucia (shown as Lucinda) Lopez and Lucia's son Henry, as well as a new child, Louisa Lopez.

The Grave of Sarah Bowman at the National Cemetery Presidio at San Francisco.
Photo courtesy Arizona Historical Society Library, Tusscon.

EPILOGUE

On 23 December 1866, at Fort Yuma, Sarah Bowman died. She was 53 years old. Edward Tuttle is the only source as to her cause of death. His memory of dates and facts was occasionally clouded. He said in his reminiscences that Sarah "built and run [sic] the first hotel in the town of Yuma in 1866, and died there the following year from the bite of a Tarantula Spider."[1] He refers to her death as being from a "poisonous spider" and a "venomous Tarantula or spider" in other versions of the same story. A tarantula bite would not normally be fatal, though some other poisonous creature would certainly be a possible cause of death.

She was buried at the Fort Yuma cemetery, the only woman ever so honored. It was the same place she had let her sheep graze four years earlier to clean out the weeds. Located on the northwest slope of the hill the fort was on, it was a lonely, quiet place. By all accounts, hers was a splendid funeral with full military honors. Tuttle was present and gave these descriptions pieced together from different letters: "The 12th Inf. at the Fort gave her a regular m litary funeral escort and all. I attended it as did everybody. The burial was in the Post Cemetery. ...The troops gave her an escort and fired a salute at her grave."[2]

Father Paul Figueroa, who left his reminiscences of early Yuma, was also there. He gave this account:

> Mrs. S. Bowman was a good hearted woman, good soul old lady of great experience, spoke the Spanish language fluently... opened the first restaurant and kept it until she died, her funeral being the first one attended in the new settlement. Her first husband had been a military man, made the military from the Post to honor her remains with a splendid funeral, with the bands and all the military observances. The vicar general was visiting the new town for the first time, and according to Catholic rite conducted the remains to the military cemetery across the river by the Fort.[3]

A story persists that Sarah was elevated to the rank of brevet colonel. The source seems to be *The Arizona Sentinel* of 13 September 1890. In the following brief history, Sarah is referred to as Mrs. Bowman-Phillips for some unknown reason.

> Mrs. Bowman-Phillips was a vivandierre [canteen manager] of the army during the Mexican War and died in Yuma in 1866. She was best known by the name of The Great Western", and was a woman of kind heart and bravery. She was breveted Colonel for services rendered in the Mexican War.

No authenticated proof for the assertion of her being given a rank exists, and it must be assumed to be in error.

The following year, in April 1867, yet another census was done in Arizona City. However, several entries are subject to question on the report.[4] Albert is listed as being "single over 21 not residing with family." As Albert and Mary did not get officially married until December of that year, he was still single when the census was taken; however, Mary was not listed anywhere on the census. It is possible that she was off visiting somewhere that day, yet it seems odd that Albert would not mention her to the census taker. Instead, beneath Albert's name is listed Henry, with ditto marks indicating his last name to be Bowman. Beneath Henry's name is that of Lucia Lopez, who earlier was noted to be living with the Bowmans in the census of 1860 and with Sarah in the census of 1866. Next is listed a child named Sarah, with ditto marks indicating a last name of Lopez. Lucia had, on the earlier censuses, been shown to have a son Henry, who is not shown on this census. Albert and Mary may have had a son out of wedlock named Henry, but it is more likely that the census taker simply made an error and placed Henry's name under Bowman instead of Lopez. It is also a curious note that Lucia now has a child named Sarah. On the census of 1866, her other child was named Louisa. She could have changed the name of her youngest child to Sarah, in honor of her recently departed friend.

Returning to the pension records submitted by Mary, she indicated that Albert lived in Yuma for nineteen years after his discharge. This would place his leaving at 1871 or 1872. Prior to his departure from Yuma, however, he was elected justice of the peace for Colorado Township on 18 October 1871.[5] M. E. Norris, the postmaster of San Antonio, Texas, stated in a letter dated 28 February 1878 that Albert had lived in San Antonio for nine months. He had previously lived "fifty miles from San Antonio at different points, for two years; previous to that time he lived in California."[6] If Norris is correct, then Albert must have stayed at the crossing until 1875. Mary gave the date and place of his death as 13 March 1882 in Pearsall, Texas. He would have been fifty-four years old. Mary was in Yuma on 25 September 1888, when she applied for a pension as a widow of a Mexican War veteran. She filed a new application in 1907 that indicated she moved to Naco, Arizona, around 1902. She continued to apply for pensions until at least 18 October 1921. Where she was at that time and when she died are unknown. In 1921, she would have been seventy-seven years old.

The fort itself lasted for seventeen years beyond Sarah's death. The Southern Pacific Railroad would be, indirectly, the final cause of its closing. When the railroad connected with Tucson from San Diego, the fort's importance was greatly reduced, as supplies could now be sent by rail to the heart of Arizona rather than the slower river route. In 1883 the fort was abandoned and government property was sold or transferred.[7]

Without soldiers or sheep to keep the cemetery clean, it became overgrown, and the 159 bodies there, including Sarah's, were forgotten. For seven long years the deterioration continued, until finally the army sent a crew on 28 August 1890 to begin exhuming and transferring the bodies to the Presidio at San Francisco. On 13 September 1890 the Arizona Sentinel ran the following article:

> The work of exhuming the remains of the soldiers in the old Fort Yuma cemetery was completed on Tuesday morning last [9 September]. The exhumation was under the immediate direction of T. B. Glover of the Quartermasters Department U. S. A. with Mr. B. F. Hartlee in charge of the working force. In all, some 159 bodies were disinterred and as considerable time had to be directed to the cleaning of the tangled and dense growth of brush and trees, the fact that but eight days were necessary for the completion of the work is worthy of remark. The remains have been shipped to the Presidio, California where they will be reinterred in the government cemetery at the post.

Another article in the same paper added the interesting note that, when Sarah's remains were exhumed, it was observed that hers were, "the largest of the many disinterred.... In the grave of the noted woman, was found a large sized medallion of metal which is the kind usually worn by Roman Catholics, the size of this one however was unusually large." So, even twenty-four years after her death, Sarah's size was still worthy of notice.

On Wednesday, 31 July 1867, the *Arizona Gazette* (Prescott), printed a copy of Sarah's obituary from "A California paper."

> She was familiarly known as the "Heroine of Fort Brown," and was at several battles during the war, caring for the wounded. Blunt and unguarded in speech, she was yet the possessor of a kind heart, and whatever her failings, engendered by wild associations, very many will remember with grateful feeling the acts of tenderness bestowed by her on themselves and associates in that inhospitable section. Al-

ways at the bedside of the sick, she cared for them as none but a woman can and nothing that money or care could furnish was neglected by her. She arrived at Fort Yuma some twelve years ago, and never could be prevailed upon to visit the limits of organized society, for which she felt her course of life had unfitted her. Brave and determined almost beyond precedent, she lost no opportunity of doing good which offered itself.... And as this mention of the decease of the "Great Western" meets the public eye, how many minds will revert to the frequent acts of kindness performed by this distinguished female representative of American frontier life, and how many an eye moisten at the remembrance of her kind attention in their hours of sickness in that isolated region.

She had lived through an incredible time of American history, and was present at the very edges of our country's expansion westward. She had been a heroine, a nurse, hospital matron, laundress, cook, camp follower, madam, wife, mother, and businesswoman. She left an impression on the great and small alike who came in contact with her, as an extraordinary woman in an extraordinary time.

Truly, she was "The Great Western."

THE END

NOTES

CHAPTER 1

1. *New Yorker*, 28 April 1838, 93.
2. W. S. Henry *Campaign Sketches Of The War With Mexico*, (New York: Harper & Brothers, 1848), 17-19.
3. John Edward Weems. *To Conquer A Peace* (Garden City, N.Y.: Doubleday, 1974), 89.
4. Ibid., 83.
5. Brantz Mayer, *History of The War Between Mexico and the United States* (New York and London: Wiley & Putnam, 1848), 1:97.
6. Ethan Allen Hitchcock, *Fifty Years In Camp And Field. Diary of Major General Ethan Allen Hitchcock, U.S.A.*, ed. W.A. Croffut (New York and London: G.P. Putnam's Sons, 1909), 207.
7. *Niles National Register* [Washington, D. C.], 15 August 1846, 373.
8. Ibid.
9. James B. O'Neil, *They Die But Once*, (New York: Knight Publishing Co., 1935), 40.
10. *Niles*, 15 August 1846, 373.
11. Lewis Leonidas Allen, *Pencillings of Scenes Upon the Rio Grande: Originally published in the Saint Louis American* (New York: N.p., 1848) [Booklet].
12. W.J.Hughes, *Rebellious Ranger: Rip Ford and the Old Southwest* (Norman, Okla.: University of Oklahoma Press, 1964) 68.
13. William H. C. Whiting, *The Journal of... Exploring Southwest Trails* ed. Ralph P.Bieber (Glendale: Arthur Clark Co., 1938), 7:309.
14. A. Russell Buchanan, "George Washington Trahern: Texan Cowboy Soldier From Mier To Buena Vista," *Southwestern Historical Quarterly* (July 1954): 60. The original is on file at the Bancroft Library, University of California, Berkeley. (Hereafter referred to as SWHQ 1954.)
15. Arthur Woodward, *The Great Western- Amazon Of The Army*, (San Francisco: Johnck and Seeger, 1961) A Clampsouvenir of the Buena Vista Chapter of the National Cemetery of San Francisco. Woodward paints a similar scenario for the origin of Sarah's nickname.
16. L. L. Allen, *Pencillings*.
17. Woodward, *Amazon*.
18. *The Decennial Federal Census, 1850 Valencia County, Territory of New Mexico*. Socorro, 320.
19. *The Decennial Federal Census, 1860 Arizona County, Territory of New Mexico*. Arizona City, 69.
20. Plot Location Card. Presidio, San Francisco.
21. G. N. Allen, *Mexican Treacheries and Cruelties...*, (Boxton and New York: N.p., 1847).
22. "Death of a Noted Female," *Arizona Gazette* [Prescott], 31 July 1867.

23. Buchanan, *SWHQ* 1954, 85.

24. Dr. J. F. Elliott makes an excellent case for Sarah's first husband being Adolfus Aue. See n. 7 of his article "The Great Western: Sarah Bowman, Mother and Mistress to the U.S. Army" which appeared in the Spring 1989 issue of the *Journal of Arizona History*.

25. A few authors, among them Dr. Arthur Woodward in his notes on the Mexican War, which were obtained from the Amon Carter Museum at Fort Worth, Texas, feel that Sarah *Foyle*, who also traveled with the army during the war, may have been one and the the same with The Great Western. In carefully reviewing Dr. Woodward's notes, and comparing dates, I have found some contradictions. Mrs. Foyle spent most of her documented time in Mexico City, but was indeed in Matamoros during the same time that The Great Western was there. Foyle remained, according to Woodward's notes, until at least November. Samuel Reid however, (see n. 2, ch. 2) spots The Great Western elsewhere in mid-September. Sarah Foyle then traveled on to Puebla and opened a store there, as she had in Matamoros. She continued on to Mexico City and opened a restaurant, theater, and hotel. In a letter to *The North American*, a newspaper published by Americans in Puebla, on 21 December 1847, Sarah Foyle describes an act of heroism whereby she claims to have captured a town called Tepeyahualco, on 20 May 1847. This would seem to conflict with Wislizenus's statement of seeing The Great Western in Saltillo on 23 May 1847, several hundred miles away (see n. 16, ch. 2). Also, Special Order No.517 of 17 June 1847 places The Great Western in Buena Vista on that date, again several hundred miles away (see n. 17, ch. 2). Added to these conflicting dates, is the fact that nowhere in the papers that Dr. Woodward refers to, is there any mention of Sarah Foyle being called The Great Western, yet our Sarah had become well known already by that name. I have not been able to locate all of the sources that Dr. Woodward cites, but the *Daily American Star* and *The North American* newspapers published by occupational forces in Mexico during the war, do not indicate any similarity between the two women other than their first name, and a similar gutsy personality. As there seems to be no positive proof that Sarah Foyle is, or is not The Great Western, I must assume that she is not.

26. L. L. Allen, *Pencillings*.

27. "The Heroine of Fort Brown," *Spirit Of The Times* [New York, 25,July 1846.

28. Mayer, *History*, 125.

29. U. S. Grant, *Personal Memoirs of U.S. Grant*. (New York: Charles L. Webster & Co., 1885), 87.

30. Lloyd Lewis, *Captain Sam Grant*, (Boston: Little, Brown & Co., 1950) 135.

31. Weems, *To Conquer*, 107.

32. *Spirit Of The Times*, 25 July 1846.

33. L. L. Allen, *Pencillings*.

34. Samuel G. French, *Two Wars: an Autobiography of Gen. Samuel G. French*, (Nashville, Tenn.: Confederate Veteran, 1901), 45.

35. Lewis, *Captain Sam Grant*, 136.

36. Henry, *Campaign Sketches*, 65.

37. Weems, *To Conquer*, 113.

38. Ben Proctor, "Fort Brown," *Frontier Forts Of Texas*, (Waco, Tex.: Texian Press, 1966), 44.

39. Ibid.

40. N. C. Brooks, *A Complete History of the Mexican War: Its Causes, Conduct, and Consequences*, (Philadelphia: Grigg, Elliot and Co., 1849) 113.

41. *Spirit Of The Times*, 25 July 1846.
42. L. L. Allen, *Pencillings*.
43. Brooks, *Complete History*, 114.
44. Proctor, "Fort Brown," 45.
45. *Spirit Of The Times*, 25 July 1846.
46. Brooks, *Complete History*, 116.
47. Ibid., 118.
48. *Spirit Of The Times*, 25 July 1846.
49. L. L. Allen, *Pencillings*.
50. Henry, *Campaign Sketches*, 103.
51. *Niles*, 4 July 1846.

CHAPTER 2

1. Samuel C. Reid Jr., *Scouting Expeditions of McCullough's Texas Rangers*, (Philadelphia: G.B. Zieber & Co., 1847), 135.
2. Nancy Hamilton, "The Great Western," in Western Writers of America, *The Women Who Made the West*, (Garden City, N. Y.: Doubleday & Co., 1980), 189.
3. Benjamin Franklin Scribner, *Camp Life of a Volunteer. A Campaign In Mexico, or a Glimpse At Life In Camp*. (1847; reprint, Austin, Tex.: Jenkins Publishing Co., 1975), 53-5.
4. Weems, *To Conquer*, 299.
5. Henry, *Campaign Sketches*, 312.
6. Ibid.
7. Buchanan, *SWHQ* 1954, 84-8.
8. Bill McGaw, "The Great Western," *The El Paso Journal* 31 December 1974.
9. G. N. Allen, *Treacheries*.
10. Ibid.
11. Sam Curtis, *Journal* (ms. on microfilm). Bancroft Library: Berkeley, Calif.
12. Ibid.
13. Edward S. Wallace, "The Great Western," *The Westerners New York Posse Brand Book*, vol. 5. no. 3, (1958): 62.
14. Frederick A. Wislizenus, *A Tour To Northern Mexico In 1846-1847*, (Glorieta, N.M.: Rio Grande Press, 1969), 75.
15. Copy of order obtained from National Archives.
16. Samuel Chamberlain, *My Confession*, (New York: Harper and Brothers, 1956) 241.
17. Ibid., 241-4.
18. Ibid., 242.
19. Ibid., 256.
20. Ibid., 256.
21. J.F. Weadock in his "Desert Notebook," which appeared in the *Daily Star* of 10 July 1961, tells of a painting of Sarah in the nude which hung above a Jerome bar. The story supposedly supposedly came to him from Dr. Arthur Woodward, but is unsubstantiated and the painting has not been located.

CHAPTER 3

1. Whiting, *Journal*, 309.
2. Rex Strickland, "Six Who Came To El Paso," *Southwestern Studies* no. 3, p. 4.
3. C. L. Sonnichsen, *Pass Of The North*, (El Paso: Texas Western Press), 124.
4. Strickland, "Six Who Came," 5.

5. John S. Ford, *Memoirs Of...* , vol. 3 p. 521. Original ms. at Barker History Center. University of Texas at Austin.
6. McGaw, "The Great Western."
7. Mary'n Rosson, "Sarah: The Great Western," *True Frontier* (April 1976): 8-11.
8. Sonnichsen, *Pass*, 126.
9. Augustus W. Knapp, "The Journal Of... ," *The Overland Monthly* (October 1887).
10. Ibid., 394.
11. Ibid.
12. Ibid.
13. Ibid., 395.
14. H. Gordon Frost, *The Gentleman's Club*, (El Paso: Mangan Books, 1983), 15.
15. C. C. Cox, "From Texas To California in 1849: The Diary of C.C. Cox." *Southwestern Historical Quarterly*, vol. 29 no.3 (January 1926): 219. Ed. by Mabelle Eppard Martin. This letter is to "a brother" by Lewis B. Harris appears in the Appendix of the article.
16. Cox, C. C. "From Texas To California in 1849: The Diary of C. C. Cox." *Southwestern Historical Quarterly* vol. 29 No. 2 (October 1925): 132.
17. *U. S. Bureau of the Census. "The Decennial Federal Census, 1850 Valencia County, Territory of New Mexico.* Socorro, 320.

CHAPTER 4

1. Pension Records, Albert Bowman. Regimental Returns of the Second Dragoons, M744, roll 16, National Archives.
2. Diary of Sylvester W. Matson, 9 May 1852, copy owned by Jerry Thompson, Laredo State University, Texas. Matson refers to her again briefly on 30 July 1852.
3. Pension Records, Albert Bowman.
4. H. B. Wharfield, *Fort Yuma On The Colorado River*, (El Cajon, Calif.: 1968), 25.
5. Wharfield, *Fort Yuma*, 47.
6. Douglas D. Martin, *Yuma Crossing*, (Albuquerque: University Of New Mexico Press, 1954), 158.
7. Ibid., 171.
8. Wharfield, *Fort Yuma*, 52.
9. James Hobbs, *Wild Life In The Far West*, (Hartford: Wiley, Waterman and Eaton, 1874), 217.
10. Diane M. T. North, *Samuel Peter Heintzelman and the Sonora Exploring and Mining Company*, (Tucson: University of Arizona Press, 1980).
11. Major Heintzelman's journal relating to this time period, is on microfilm at the Arizona Historical Foundation at Arizona State University in Tempe. The entire original manuscript is on microfilm at the Library of Congress. This entry is from 10 October 1853. Hereafter designated as HJ.
12. Ibid., 12 October 1853.
13. Ibid., 14 October 1853.
14. Ibid., 15 October 1853.
15. Ibid., 26 October 1853.
16. Ibid., 22 November 1853.
17. Ibid., 29 November 1853.
18. Ibid., 24 December 1853.
19. Ibid., 4 January 1854.
20. Ibid., 5 January 1854.

21. Ibid., 12 January 1854.
22. Ibid., 18 January 1854.
23. Ibid., 30 January 1854.
24. Ibid., 31 January 1854.
25. Ibid., 1 February 1854.
26. Ibid.
27. Ibid., 8 February 1854.
28. Ibid., 12 February 1854.
29. Ibid., 1 March 1854.
30. Ibid., 3 March 1854.
31. Ibid., 5 March 1854.
32. Ibid., 6 March 1854.
33. Ibid., 14 March 1854.
34. Ibid., 21 March 1854.
35. Ibid., 22 March 1854.
36. Ibid., 23 March 1854.
37. Ibid., 1 April 1854.
38. Ibid., 2 April 1854.
39. Ibid., 4 April 1854.
40. Ibid., 5 April 1854.
41. Ibid., 9 April 1854.
42. Ibid., 11 April 1854.
43. Ibid., 19 April 1854.
44. Ben Sacks, cardfile at Arizona Historical Foundation, Arizona State University in Tempe. The Sacks cardfile contains thousands of cards that are crossreferenced to thousands of other hand-copied sheets relating to Arizona history. The section headed "The Great Western" contains more than one hundred cards full of references and notes.
45. HJ, 21 April 1854.
46. Ibid., 22 April 1854.
47. Ibid.
48. Ibid., 23 April 1854.
49. Ibid., 29 April 1854.
50. Ibid., 3 May 1854.
51. Ibid., 9 May 1854.
52. Ibid., 23 May 1854.
53. Ibid., 29 May 1854.
54. Ibid., 9 June 1854.
55. Ibid., 17 June 1854.
56. Ibid., 23 June 1854.
57. Ibid., 8 July 1854.
58. Ibid., 14 July 1854.

CHAPTER 5

1. Thomas Edwin Farish, *History of Arizona*, (San Francisco: Filmer Brothers Electrotype Co., 1915), 1:189.
2. Ibid., 1:329.
3. HJ, 11 July 1854.
4. Farish, *History*, 1:321.

5. Record of Claims A, La Paz District, Ariz. 142-44, AHF.
6. Ibid., 192-94.
7. Book 12 QMGO contracts of 1852, 196, Sacks Collection, AHF.
8. Notecards of Albert Bowman, Sacks Collection.
9. Wharfield, *Fort Yuma*, 81.
10. William Mulder and A. Russell Mortensen, *Among The Mormons*, (New York: Alfred A. Knopf, 1958), 277.
11. Western Americana Collection of the Yale University Library, New Haven, Conn. The letter is reprinted in *The Westerners New York Posse Brand Book*, vol. 15, no. 2, 1968. Hereafter designated Mowry letter.
12. Ibid.
13. Ibid.
14. Marshall Trimble, Arizona, (Garden City, N. Y.: Doubleday & Co., 1977), 217.
15. George William Beattie, "Diary of a Ferryman and Trader at Fort Yuma 1855-1857," *Historical Society of Southern California Journal*, (Los Angeles: McBride Publishing Co., 1928), 89.
16. Ibid., 95.
17. Ibid., 101.
18. R. B. Stratton, Captivity of the Oatman Girls, (1857; reprint, Lincoln: University of Nebraska Press, 1983).
19. Charles D. Poston, "The Oatman Family," *Phoenix Daily Herald*, 6 June 1891.
20. Edward Tuttle, "Papers of...". Special Collections, University of Arizona Library, Tucson.
21. Edward J. Pettid, "The Oatman Story," *Arizona Highways* (November 1968): 4-9.
22. Beattie, "Diary," 111-115.
23. Solomon Warner Collection, box 6, folder 59, Arizona Historical Society, Tucson. Pertinent entries are in a ledger on pp.22, 49, 60.
24. Pima County Deeds of Real Estate, book 1, p.10, microfilm, Sacks Collection, AHF.
25. Pension Records of Albert Bowman, National Archives.
26. Henry P. Walker and Don Bufkin, *Historical Atlas of Arizona*, (Norman: University of Oklahoma Press, 1979), 26.
27. Pima County Deeds of Real Estate, book 1, p.10.
28. James B. O'Neil, *They Die But Once*, (New York: Knight Publications, 1935), 29-30.
29. Solomon Warner Collection, AHS.
30. Trimble, *Arizona*, 218.
31. *The Decennial Federal Census of 1860*. Arizona County, Territory of New Mexico, 69.
32. O'Neil, *They Die*, 40.
33. Raphael Pumpelly, *My Reminiscences*, (New York: Henry Holt & Co., 1918), 258-59.
34. Wharfield, *Fort Yuma*, 139.
35. Ibid., 138.
36. George H. Pettis, *Frontier Service During The Rebellion*, (Providence, R. I.;1885), 18.
37. Wharfield, *Fort Yuma*, 142.
38. Tuttle, "Papers."
39. Ibid.
40. Special Territorial Census of 1864, taken in Arizona, State Archives, Phoenix.
41. The Sacks Collection at AHF has many cards relating to Bowman which list many mines he was involved with in varying capacities. Several record books are listed as references.

42. "Fort Yuma Investigations 1862-3", Sacks File, AHF.
43. This document is in a report from Col. N. H. Davis, and is also found in Sacks file: "Fort Yuma Investigations — 1864."
44. Sacks file, AHF.
45. U. S. Census, Special Arizona Enumeration, 1866.
46. Pension Records of Albert Bowman.

EPILOGUE

1. Tuttle, "Papers."
2. Ibid.
3. Paul Figueroa, ms., Arizona Historical Society, Tucson.
4. U. S. Census, Special Arizona Enumeration, 1867, AHF.
5. A document entitled "Certificate of Election," filed in San Diego County 18 October 1871, was included with copies received of Bowman's Bounty Land Application from the National Archives.
6. This letter was also included with the Bounty Land Application from the National Archives.
7. Wharfield, *Fort Yuma*, 176.

BIBLIOGRAPHY

BOOKS

Abernethy, Francis Edward. *Legendary Ladies of Texas*. Dallas: E-Heart Pess, 1980.

Allen, G. N. *Mexican Treacheries and Cruelties, Incidents and Sufferings in the Mexican War; with accounts of hardships endured; treacheries of the Mexicans; battles fought, and success of American arms; also, an account of valiant soldiers fallen, and the particulars of the death and funeral services in honor of Capt. George Lincoln of Worcesters"*. Boston and New York, 1847.

Allen, L. L. *Pencillings of Scenes Upon The Rio Grande: Originally published in The Saint Louis American*. New York, 1848.

Barbour, Philip Norbourne, and Isabella Hopkins Barbour. *Journals of the Late Brevet Major... and his wife...* Edited by Rhoda van Bibber Tanner Doubleday. New York: G. P. Putnam's Sons, 1936.

Barney, James. *Yuma*. (Booklet) Charter Oak Insurance Co., 1953.

Branda, Eldon Stephen, ed. *The Handbook of Texas*. Vol. 3. Austin: Texas State Historical Association, 1976.

Brooks, N. C. *A Complete History of the Mexican War: Its Causes, Conduct, and Consequences 1849*. Chicago: The Rio Grande Press, 1965.

Browne, J. Ross. *Adventures in the Apache Country: A Tour Through Arizona and Sonora, 1864.1869*. Reprint. Tucson: University of Arizona Press, 1974.

Chamberlain, Samuel E. *My Confession*. New York: Harper and Brothers, 1956.

Crowe, Rosalie, and Sidney B. Brinckerhoff. *Early Yuma. A Graphic History of Life on the American Nile*. Flagstaff: Northland Press, 1976.

Egan, Ferrol. *The El Dorado Trail: The Story of the Gold Rush Routes Across Mexico*. New York: McGraw-Hill, 1970.

Farish, Thomas Edwin. *History of Arizona*. 8 vols. San Francisco: Filmer Brothers Electrotype Co., 1915.

French, Samuel G. *Two Wars: An Autobiography of Gen. Samuel G. French*. Nashville: Confederate Veteran, 1901.

Frost, H. Gordon. *The Gentleman's Club: The Story of Prostitution in El Paso*. El Paso: Mangan Books, 1983.

Granger, Byrd Howell. *Arizona's Names (X Marks the Place)*. Tucson: Falconer Publishing Co., 1983.

Grant, U. S. *Personal Memoirs of....* 2 vols. New York, 1885.

Haley, J. Evetts. *Fort Concho and the Texas Frontier*. San Angelo, Tex.: San Angelo Standard-Times, 1952.

Hamilton, Nancy. "The Great Western." In Western Writers of America, *Women Who Made The West*. Garden City, N. Y.: Doubleday and Co., 1980.

Hart, Herbert M. *Old Forts of the West*. Seattle: Superior Publishing Co., 1965.

Henry, W. S. *Campaign Sketches of the War with Mexico*. New York, 1848.
Hitchcock, Ethan Allen. *Fifty Years in Camp and Field: The Diary of Major-General Ethan Allen Hitchcock, U.S.A.*. Edited by W. A. Croffut. New York: G. P. Putnam's Sons, 1909.
Hobbs, James. *Wild Life In The Far West; Personal Adventures Of a Border Mountain Man*. Hartford, 1874.
Hughes, W. J. *Rebellious Ranger: Rip Ford and the Old Southwest*. Norman: University of Oklahoma Press, 1964.
Johannsen, Robert W. *To The Halls of the Montezumas: The Mexican War in the American Imagination*. New York: Oxford University Press, 1985.
Lewis, Lloyd. *Captain Sam Grant*. Boston: Little, Brown & Co., 1950.
Love, Frank. *From Brothel To Boomtown: Yuma's Naughty Past*. Colorado Springs: Little London Press, 1981.
Maddocks, Melvin, and the editors of Time-Life Books. *The Great Liners*. Seafarers series. Alexandria, Va.: Time-Life Books, 1982.
Martin, Douglas D. *Yuma Crossing*. Albuquerque: University of New Mexico Press, 1954.
Mayer, Brantz. *History of the War Between Mexico and the United States*. 2 vols. New York and London, 1848.
Metz, Leon C. *Turning Points in El Paso Texas*. El Paso: Mangan Books, 1985.
Miller, Ronald Dean. *Shady Ladies of the West*. Los Angeles: Westernlore Press, 1964.
Mulder, William, and A. Russell Mortensen eds. *Among the Mormons: Historic Accounts by Contemporary Observers*. New York: Alfred A. Knopf, 1958.
Myers, John Myers. *Deaths Of The Bravos*. Boston: Little, Brown & Co., 1962.
North, Diane M. T. *Samuel Peter Heintzelman and the Sonora Exploring and Mining Company*. Tucson: University of Arizona Press, 1980.
O'Neil, James B. *They Die But Once: The Story of a Tejano*. New York: Knight Publications, 1935.
Pettis, George H. *Frontier Service During The Rebellion*. Providence, R.I., 1885
Pumpelly, Raphael. *My Reminiscences*. New York: Henry Holt & Co., 1918.
Proctor, Ben. "Fort Brown". In *Frontier Forts of Texas*. Waco: Texian Prss, 1966.
Reid, Samuel C., Jr. *The Scouting Expeditions of McCullough's Texas Rangers.*. Philadelphia, 1847.
Sacks, Ben. *Be It Enacted: The Creation of the Territory of Arizona*. Phoenix: Arizona Historical Foundation, 1964.
Scribner, Benjamin Franklin. *Camp Life of a Volunteer: A Campaign in Mexico or a Glimpse at Life in Camp*. 1847. Reprint. Austin: Jenkins Publishing Co., 1975.
Smith, E. Kirby. *To Mexico With Scott: Letters of Captain E. Kirby Smith To His Wife*. Camridge: Harvard University Press, 1917.
Smith, George Winston, and Charles Judah, eds. *Chronicles of The Gringos: The U. S. Army in the Mexican War, 1846-1848 Accounts of Eyewitnesses and Combatants*. Albuquerque: University of New Mexico Press, 1968.
Sonnichsen, C. L. *Pass Of the North: Four Centuries On The Rio Grande*. El Paso: Texas Western Press, 1968.
Stratton, R. B. *Captivity of the Oatman Girls*. 1857. Reprint. Lincoln: University of Nebraska Press, 1983.
Trimble, Marshall. *Arizona: A Panoramic History Of A Frontier State*. Garden City, N.Y.: Doubleday, 1977.

_____. *Roadside History of Arizona.* Missoula: Mountain Press Publishing Co., 1986.
Wallace, Edward S. *The Great Reconnaissance.* Boston: Little, Brown & Co., 1955.
Walker, Henry P., and Don Bufkin. *Historical Atlas of Arizona.* Norman: University of Oklahoma Press, 1979.
Weems, John Edward. *To Conquer A Peace: The War Between the United States and Mexico.* Garden City, N.Y.: Doubleday, 1974.
Wharfield, H. B. *Fort Yuma On the Colorado River.* El Cajon, Calif., 1968.
Whiting, William H. C. *Journal of... Exploring Southwest Trails.* Vol. 7. Edited by Ralph Bieber. Glendale: Arthur Clark Co., 1938.
Wislizenus, Frederick A. *A Tour To Northern Mexico in 1846-1847.* Glorieta, N. M.: The Grande Press, 1969.
Woodward, Arthur. *The Great Western: Amazon of the Army.* San Francisco: Johnck and Seeger, 1961.

NEWSPAPERS

Arizona Daily Star [Tucson], 10 July 1961.
Arizona Gazette [Prescott], 31 July 1867.
Arizona Republic, 24 Mar. 1985, 14 April 1942.
Arizona Sentinel [Yuma], 13 Sept. 1890, 25 Aug. 1877.
Arizona Sun [Yuma]. 10 June 1960.
Daily American Star [Mexico City]. Various issues 1847-8.
El Paso Herald-Post, 24 Oct. 1956, 14 July 1976, 28 May 1936.
The El Paso Journal, 31 Dec.
The New Yorker, 28 April 1838.
Niles National Register [Philadelphia], 4 July 1846, 15 Aug. 1846.
The North American [Mexico City]. Various issues 1847-8.
Phoenix Daily Herald, 6 June 1891.
San Diego Herald, 3 Oct. 1857.
Spirit Of The Times [New York], 25 July 1846.

MAGAZINES AND JOURNALS

Sacks, Ben. "Sylvester Mowry." *American West Magazine* (Summer 1964): 14-24, 79.
Bloom, John Porter. "'Johnny Gringo' In Northern Mexico, 1846- 1847." *Arizona and the West* (Autumn 1962): 237-248.
Beattie, George William. "Diary of a Ferryman and Trader at Fort Yuma, 1855-1857." *Historical Society of Southern California Journal* vol. 19 Part 1 (1928): 89.
Elliott, J. F. "The Great Western: Sarah Bowman, Mother and Mistress to the U. S. Army." *The Journal of Arizona History* 30, no. 1 (Spring 1989).
Roberts, Virginia Cullen. "Heroines on the Arizona Frontier: The First Anglo-American Women." *The Journal of Arizona History* 23, No. 1 (Spring 1982).
Woodward, Arthur. "The Great Western." *Los Angeles Westerners Corral* (June 1956).
Griffith, A. Kinney. "The Most Dangerous Game: The Hunters and the Hunted." *Old West Magazine* (Spring 1965): 4-9, 54-55.
Knapp, Augustus W. "An Old Californian's Pioneer Story." *The Overland Monthly* (October 1887): 394-95.
Barney, James M. "The Story Of 'The Great Western'." *Sheriff Magazine* (March 1954): 24-25.
Ferguson, H. N. "The Great Western." *Texas Parade* (January 1959): 14-15.

Canning, Margaret H. "The Great Western." *Tradition* (April 1959): 84-88.
Rosson, Mary'n. "Sarah: The Great Western." *True Frontier* (April 1976): 8-11.
McGaw, Bill. "Great Western A Big Beauty Who Could Whip A Man Or Simply Love Him To Death." *The Southwesterner* (August 1967): 1, 12.
Woodward, Arthur. "'Great Western' Was Earliest Inn-Keeper In Old El Paso- You Could Call Her Madam." *The Southwesterner* (August 1963).
Buchanan, A. Russell, ed. "George Washington Trahern: Texan Cowboy Soldier From Mier To Buena Vista." *The Southwestern Historical Quarterly*, 58, no. 1 (July 1954).
Martin, Mabelle Eppard, ed. "From Texas To California In 1849: Diary of C. C. Cox." *The Southwestern Historical Quarterly* 29, no. 2 (July 1925), and 29, no. 3 (January 1926).
Strickland, Rex W. "Six Who Came To El Paso: Pioneers Of The 1840's." *Southwestern Studies* 1, no. 3 (Fall 1963).
Josephy, Alvin M., Jr. "Two Gamy Letters From Fort Yuma." *The Westerners: New York Posse Brand Book* 15, no. 2 (1968), 26.
Wallace, Edward S. "The Great Western." *The Westerners: New York Posse Brand Book* 5, no. 3 (1958), 758.
Ainsworth, Ed. "Posse In Search Of A Ghost." *Westways* (Febrary 1956): 14.

OTHER SOURCES

Amon Carter Museum at Fort Worth, Texas:
Woodward, Arthur. *Papers of....* Have copies of Woodward's notes relating to the Mexican War, which include quite a bit about Sarah. The Arizona Historical Society in Tucson has the originals, however they are not, as yet, available for use.
Arizona Historical Foundation at A.S.U. Library, Tempe:
Heintzelman, Samuel P. *Journal of....* On several rolls of microfilm in the Sacks Collection.
Sacks, Ben. *Collection*. Includes notecards, microfilm, handcopied and xeroxed "sheets" and files. This also includes a file marked "E. S. Wallace", in which Dr. Sacks retained copies of his correspondence with Wallace regarding "The Great Western."
Record of Claims book "A." La Paz District, Arizona. Sacks Collection files have copy.
Fort Yuma investigations. Sacks Collection. Originals from Record Group 98, National Archives.
Decennial Federal Census in the County of Arizona, Territory of New Mexico. Arizona City p. 69. On Microfilm at AHF.
Federal Census, Special Arizona Enumeration 1866. Yuma County, Arizona City. Arizona Historical Foundation has copy.
Federal Census, Special Arizona Enumeration 1867. Yuma County, Arizona City. Arizona Historical Foundation has copy.
Arizona Historical Society Library, Tucson:
Figueroa, Paul. (Manuscript).
Warner, Solomon. *Collection*.
Arizona State Archives:
Elliot, J. F. *Sarah Bowman — The Great Western* ts. Submitted to the Arizona State Archives office with a nomination for Sarah's admission to the Arizona Women's Hall of Fame.
Federal Census, Special Arizona Enumeration 1864. Second Judicial District, Arizona City. Original at Arizona State Archives, Phoenix.
National Archives and Records Administration:
Albert Bowman's service and pension records.

Record Group 94: Records of the Adjutant Generals Office. Entry 44: Orders and Circulars, Army of Occupation, Mexican War. General Wool's Orders, Vol. 39. Special Order 517, dated 17 June 1847.

Regimental Returns of 2nd Dragoons for the period of interest are available on microfilm number M-744, roll 16.

New Mexico Records Center and Archives:

Decennial Federal Census of New Mexico, 1850, Valencia Co. (Socorro) p.319 and 320. Microfilm edition copy.

University of Arizona Special Collections Library, Tucson:

Tuttle, Edward. *Papers of....* Original at Huntington Library, San Marino, California.

University of California at Berkeley, Bancroft Library:

Curtis, Samuel Ryan Papers (N-M 1723).

Trahern, George Washington. Dictation and biographical sketch, n. d. (C-D 843).

University of Texas at Austin, Barker History Center:

Ford, John S. *Memoirs of....* Vol. 3, 1846-1851. Manuscript #235867.